ANSWERS

Answers

Catholic Advice
for Your Spiritual Questions

Father John Bartunek, L.C., S.T.D.

SERVANT
BOOKS

PUBLISHED BY FRANCISCAN MEDIA
Cincinnati, Ohio

Cover and book design by Mark Sullivan

Cover image © Burak Çakmak | Veer

LIBRARY OF CONGRESS CATALOGING-IN-PUBLICATION DATA

Bartunek, John.

Answers : Catholic advice for your spiritual questions /
Father John Bartunek, L.C., S.T.D.

pages cm

Includes bibliographical references.

ISBN 978-1-61636-822-7 (alk. paper)

1. Christian life—Catholic authors—Miscellanea. 2. Catholic Church—Doctrines.—Miscellanea. 3. Theology, Doctrinal—Popular works. I. Title.

BX2350.3.B377 2014

230'.2—dc23

2014016008

ISBN 978-1-61636-822-7

Published by Servant Books, an imprint of Franciscan Media

28 W. Liberty St.

Cincinnati, OH 45202

www.FranciscanMedia.org

Printed in the United States of America.

Printed on acid-free paper.

14 15 16 17 18 5 4 3 2 1

Contents

Foreword

THE ADVENTURE OF THE HUMAN spirit radiates with glory when God is the midst of the struggle for clarity and purpose. In this struggle, for the sincere and thoughtful pilgrim, questions never cease rising to the surface:

"Why is there so much suffering?"

"Does God love me?"

"How can I know God?"

"What is prayer?"

"Will God speak to me in prayer?"

"What makes Catholicism different?"

Properly aimed and answered, these questions can launch the soul into an engagement with God that it would have otherwise never known. It is in this powerful exchange of questions and answers that Fr. John Bartunek and I engaged with thousands of faithful pilgrims from all over the world.

The project began in 2009 when I asked Fr. John to join me on what I thought might have an effect on a small number of those seeking answers. Instead, just a few years later, we have touched every inhabited country of the world and, in the midst of it all, created the largest online community dedicated to the divine dialogue of hearts seeking ultimate answers.

Hundreds of thousands of God-seekers visit the Roman Catholic Spiritual Direction website (RCSpiritualDirection.com) every year. The surprising thing about this dialogue is how interesting and engaging it is even for those who are only marginally concerned with the musings and wrestling with eternal realities. Why the interest? Because even for those souls who have yet to fully engage, all have an innate desire for God—a desire for higher purpose and meaning. Here's how the *Catechism of the Catholic Church* states this reality:

> The desire for God is written in the human heart, because man is created by God and for God; and God never ceases to draw man to himself. Only in God will he find the truth and happiness he never stops searching for:
>
> The dignity of man rests above all on the fact that he is called to communion with God. This invitation to converse with God is addressed to man as soon as he comes into being. For if man exists, it is because God has created him through love, and through love continues to hold him in existence. He cannot live fully according to truth unless he freely acknowledges that love and entrusts himself to his creator. (*CCC* 27)

In this sacred searching, these great themes are explored not in an abstract or theoretical way but in a gritty, down-to-earth, practical way that anyone can relate to. Within this fascinating formula of questions and answers and ensuing engagement, lives have been changed, hearts renewed and restored to faith, hope, and love. This is the power of leaning into the unknown that ignites the hearts of all who peer in.

Fr. John has done a great service to the Church. He has given his life to helping anyone within his reach understand what it means to be in authentic relationship with God. This book and the realities proposed within it will change your life, if you will only lean in and never stop asking and seeking.

> Thus says the Lord: "Stand by the roads, and look,
> and ask for the ancient paths,
> where the good way is; and walk in it,
> and find rest for your souls. (Jeremiah 6:16)

—Dan Burke, executive director of EWTN's *National Catholic Register*

Chapter One

Prayer

IN TODAY'S WORLD, WHICH IS so fast-paced, noisy, and distracting, it's more important than ever to carve out quiet time to be alone with God, to reflect on the deep Catholic truths that nourish our souls. It's no longer enough simply to attend Mass on Sunday—at least, not if we really want to reach maturity in our Christian lives. Society no longer supports Christian values or worldview as it once did, so we need to intentionally create space for the Holy Spirit to give us the support we need directly. Whether you are a beginner or a veteran in prayer, if you sincerely want to go deeper in your prayer life, I hope the answers in this chapter will prove useful to you.

HOW CAN I HEAR GOD SPEAKING TO ME IN PRAYER?

The phrase "conversation with God" describes Christian prayer beautifully. Christ has revealed that God is a real person, and that he is interested—passionately interested—in our lives, our friendship, our closeness. For Christians then, prayer, as Pope Benedict explained when he visited Yonkers, New York, in 2007, is an expression of our "personal relationship with God." And that relationship, the Holy Father went on to say, "is what matters most."

Parameters of Faith

When we pray, God speaks to us. First of all, though, we need to remember that our relationship with God is based on faith. Faith gives us access to knowledge that goes beyond what we can perceive by our senses. By faith, for example, we know that Christ is truly present in the Eucharist, even though our senses only perceive the appearances of bread and wine. Whenever a Christian prays, the prayer takes place within this atmosphere of faith.

When I address God in vocal prayer, I know that he is listening to me, even if I don't feel his presence with my senses or emotions. When I praise him, ask things of him, adore him, thank him, tell him I am sorry…in all these expressions of prayer, I know by faith (not necessarily by my senses or my feelings) that God is listening, interested, and that he cares. If we try to understand Christian prayer outside of this atmosphere of faith, we will get nowhere.

Keeping that in mind, let's look at the three ways God speaks to us in prayer.

1. The Gift of Consolation

First of all, God can speak to us by giving us what spiritual writers call *consolation*. Through consolation, he touches the soul and allows it to be comforted and strengthened by a felt awareness of his love, his presence, his goodness, his power, and his beauty.

This consolation can flow directly from the meaning of the words of a vocal prayer. For instance, when I pray Blessed Cardinal Newman's famous "Lead, Kindly Light" prayer, God may boost my hope and confidence, simply because the meaning of the words nourish and revitalize my awareness of God's power and goodness.

Consolation can also flow from the reflection and pondering involved in mental prayer. As I read and reflect slowly, prayerfully on the parable of the Prodigal Son, for example, I can feel my soul being comforted by that picture of the Father embracing the repentant younger brother. That picture of God's love comes to my mind, and it gives me a renewed awareness of God's mercy and goodness. *God is so merciful!* I think to myself, and I feel the warmth of his mercy in my heart. That image and those ideas are mine, insofar as they arise in my mind, but they are from God, insofar as they arose in *response* to my consideration of *God's revelation*, in an atmosphere of faith.

Or, on another occasion, I could meditate on the same biblical passage and be moved to a deep experience of sorrow for my own sins: in the ungrateful rebellion of the Prodigal Son, I see an image of my own sins and rebellions, and I am repelled by them. Again, the idea of the ugliness of sin and the feeling of sorrow for my personal sins are my own ideas and feelings, but they are a *response to God's action* in my mind as he guides my mind's eye to perceive certain aspects of his truth while I listen to him speaking through his revealed Word in the Bible.

In any of these cases, my soul is touched anew, and thus nourished and consoled, by the truth of who God is for me, and who I am for him—a truth which God speaks to my soul. But the distinction between God's speaking and my own ideas is not so clear as we would sometimes like. He actually speaks *through* the ideas that come as I turn my attention toward him in prayer. He speaks within my heart, within the words that form in my heart as I gaze at the Word.

2. Nourishing the Gifts of the Holy Spirit

In the second place, God can respond to us in prayer by increasing the gifts of the Holy Spirit in our souls: wisdom, knowledge, understanding, piety, fear of the Lord, fortitude, and counsel. Each of these gifts nourishes our spiritual muscles, so to speak; they build up our spiritual faculties. They make it easier for us to discover God's will in our lives, to appreciate and want his will, and to carry out that will. In short, they enhance our ability to believe, to hope, and to love God and neighbor. During a time of prayer, then, when I am addressing God in vocal prayer, or seeking to know him more deeply through mental prayer, or adoring him through liturgical prayer, God's grace touches my soul, nourishing it through increasing the power of these gifts of the Holy Spirit.

Since these gifts are spiritual, and not material, and since God's grace is spiritual, I will not always feel the nourishing take place. I may spend fifteen minutes reading and reflecting on the parable of the Good Shepherd, and no consoling ideas or feelings are stirred up; my prayer feels dry. But that doesn't mean that God's grace is not nourishing my soul, that he is not strengthening within me the gifts of the Holy Spirit.

When I take vitamins (or eat broccoli), I don't feel my muscles grow, but I know that those vitamins are indeed enabling that growth. Likewise, when we pray, we know we are entering into contact with God's grace, with a God who loves us and is making us holy. When I don't experience consolation, I can be certain that God is still working in my soul, strengthening it with his gifts by means of the spiritual vitamins that my soul takes in whenever I have faith-filled contact with God. But I only know this by faith, because God doesn't always send sensible consolation with this spiritual nourishment. This is why spiritual growth depends so significantly on our perseverance in prayer, regardless of whether we feel consolation.

3. Direct Inspirations

Third, God can speak to our souls through words, ideas, or inspirations that we recognize clearly as coming right from him. Personally, I have a vivid memory of the first time the thought of the priesthood came into my mind. I wasn't even Catholic yet. No one had told me that I should become a priest. And yet, in the aftermath of a powerful spiritual experience, the thought simply appeared in my mind, fully formed, with compelling clarity. I knew without any doubt that the thought had come directly from God, that he had spoken to me directly, giving me an inspiration.

Most of us have had some, if only a few, experiences like this, when we knew God was saying something specific to us, even though we heard the words only in our hearts and not with our physical ears. God can speak in this way even when we are not at prayer. But a mature prayer life will make our souls more sensitive to these direct inspirations, and create more room for God to speak directly more often, if he wishes to do so.

Jesus assured us that any effort we make in prayer will bring grace into our souls, whether we feel it or not: "Seek, and you shall find; ask, and it shall be given to you; knock, and the door will be opened" (Matthew 7:7–8). But at the same time, we have to always remember that we must live our entire lives, including our prayer lives, in the light of our faith, not only in accordance with what we perceive and with what we feel. As St. Paul said so powerfully, "We walk by faith, not by sight" (2 Corinthians 5:7).

WHAT IS THE DIFFERENCE BETWEEN CONTEMPLATION AND MEDITATION?

Contemplative prayer consists of a more passive (and more sublime) experience of God. If Christian meditation is the soul's inspired quest to discover God (our work of seeking God), contemplation is God's lifting of the soul into himself (God's work of embrace), so that it effortlessly basks in the divine light. The key distinction here is that contemplation, in the strict sense, is purely the work of God. Meditation, though aided by God and predicated upon the grace and work of Christ, is the result of our seeking him. That basic distinction is often blurred, causing confusion, because both contemplation and meditation take multiple forms.

In general, meditative prayer is mostly *discursive* or mostly *affective*. A discursive meditation follows a more logical development, analyzing a truth of the faith or a Scripture passage in order to discover an insight or deepen one's Christian understanding. That discovery or deepening leads the soul out of analysis and reflection and into conversation with God— acts of thanksgiving, praise, contrition, or petition. An affective meditation puts less emphasis on analysis or reflection, and more emphasis on the conversation, the acts of thanksgiving and praise that flow from the soul's spiritual (not necessarily emotional) affections. Sometimes a mere glance at a biblical phrase can stir up a strong affection in the soul, and that is enough for the soul to enter into conversation with God; this is primarily an affective meditation. Other times, a long period of reflection, of analytical searching, finally yields an affection that leads to conversation; this is a mostly discursive meditation.

In certain seasons of the spiritual life, especially as the soul increases in spiritual maturity, meditation naturally becomes more affective. When a soul finds itself regularly and easily entering into contact with God, with hardly any discursive effort, this is often called the "prayer of quiet" or the "prayer of simplicity." The soul finds itself easily gazing silently at the grandeur of God. Because so little effort is required in this kind of almost exclusively affective meditation, it is often called contemplative prayer.

This is a common and valid use of the term. But it can cause confusion, because in a strict sense, and in the writings of mystics and theologians, contemplative prayer ("infused contemplation" is the technical term) goes even beyond this adoring gaze. We can gaze at the ocean and experience a deep sense of wonder, but it is another thing altogether to be submerged in the water. Infused contemplation is when God submerges us in himself; we no long gaze at God from without, but experience an ineffable union with him. Think of a piece of iron that is thrust into the fire and takes on the qualities of the fire.

And so, the most active type of mental prayer (as opposed to vocal prayer) is discursive meditation, which dovetails with affective meditation, which in turn culminates in the prayer of quiet, in which the soul enters effortlessly into extended acts of thanksgiving, praise, contrition, or petition. This is so effortless that it is akin to and often called contemplation. Infused contemplation, however, actually goes to a new level, lifting the soul out of itself and into the divine.

HOW CAN I PRACTICE THE PRESENCE OF GOD?

"Practicing the presence of God" means staying aware of Jesus throughout the day, but that's only part of it. Practicing God's presence means living every activity of the day *with* Jesus, by his side, sharing every experience with him. Remember how, in your school days, it was always more enjoyable to do your homework with a good friend instead of all by yourself? You didn't have to be doing the exact same assignments, and you didn't even have to be helping each other, but the mere fact that you were together, sitting in the same room, maybe at the same table, that you were in each other's presence and could throw a couple words or looks back and forth every once awhile was enough to change the character of doing homework.

Think of another example. How often do you go to a movie all by yourself? Most likely not very often, unless you are a professional movie critic. You usually go to a movie with a good friend or family member. And even though you don't spend those two hours talking with each other, sharing the experience with another person makes the experience more valuable, fruitful, and enjoyable. This sharing of experiences—the experience of every activity of every day—with Christ, allowing him to share the experience of your life, that is the real heart of "practicing the presence of God."

The Effect in Our Lives

As we grow in this spiritual discipline, it has a major effect on our lives. We were created to "live in communion with God, in whom we find happiness" (*CCC* 45). But in this fallen world and due to our fallen nature, we tend toward a false sense of self-sufficiency. This stifles our growth as human beings. Instead of growing in wisdom, wonder, courage, and all the other virtues, when we live as if we were sufficient unto ourselves, we end up taking the path that eventually turns us into crotchety old men (or women), self-absorbed and self-absorbing, like black holes. Practicing the presence of God helps us maintain and deepen our communion with

God even in the midst of the trials and tribulations of life in a fallen world with a fallen human nature. This is the path to holiness (God's term for lasting happiness).

Principles for Practicing

Since everyone's friendship with God is unique, no generic formula will suffice for developing this spiritual discipline. Nevertheless, some common principles apply to all of us.

First of all, we need to develop the basic spiritual disciplines: a structured and consistent daily prayer life (this doesn't have to be as complicated as a monastic prayer life, just sincere and substantial); regular and fruitful reception of the sacraments, especially Communion and confession (this is the objective foundation of our communion with God— God's grace is the stuff of which our friendship with Christ is made); and a reasonable, mature effort to overcome one's selfish tendencies and to grow in virtue (spiritual reading, a program of life, and spiritual direction are a big help here, as mentioned before).

Second, we can experiment with practical techniques that will help us form the habit of remembering that we are never alone, that Jesus is at our side, eager to share our experiences and make them fruitful and meaningful. Here is where tactics like the spiritual bouquet come into play (choosing a phrase at the end of the morning meditation that you will use as a motto for the day, to keep in mind the insights and resolutions that came up in your meditation). You can also get creative: using a screen saver that will remind you of the Lord; keeping religious articles visible in key places that you will frequent during the day; programming reminders into your email calendar; praying the Angelus whenever you get into the car to go for a drive; or dropping by a local shrine, chapel, or church on your way home from work, school, or shopping.

Since the current of the culture in which we live flows in the direction of self-centeredness and self-absorption, we have to make a positive effort to swim against it. Practical tactics can help. But here's a warning: these are only means to an end, so don't be surprised if one such tactic helps you for a while but then stops working. When that happens, experiment with something else.

Third, and most important, ask yourself why it has been difficult for you to practice the presence of God. Part of the reason will simply be the superficiality and pace of our culture. Part of the reason will also be habits of self-centeredness that you haven't yet overcome. But a deeper reason may also be at work. When you go to a dinner party with people who are important, fashionable, and popular, but who you don't know very well, you are a bit nervous. You are worried about making the right impression. You don't want to commit a *faux pas* or inadvertently offend someone. You are excited to be invited, but the excitement is mixed in with some tension. Whether things go well or ill, at the end of the night, when you get back in the car to head home, you breathe a sigh of relief; driving home with your spouse or with an old friend, you can be yourself again. At the party you were sharing experiences with people, you were living in their presence, but you didn't have a relationship of trust with them. With your old friend, on the other hand, you never have to worry about making a good impression; you don't have to be anxious about what they may think of you. Your relationship is solid, resilient, familiar—you can relax together.

At times, the biggest obstacle to our practicing the presence of God is a subtle, subconscious fear about what God thinks of us. In the back of our mind, we are concerned about making the right impression in God's eyes, and so when we are in his presence, we put on a show; we watch carefully over every word instead of speaking simply and from the heart; we try to live up to standards we imagine God is expecting of us; we are afraid that if we don't meet those extra expectations, God will be displeased with us—he won't invite us back to the next party. This mindset discourages us from living in God's presence, because we can't relax and be ourselves if we are trying to live up to artificial expectations.

But God is not like that. He is not watching us like a hawk, just waiting for that *faux pas*, just looking for something to criticize. He knows us through and through already. He truly is the only friend who is perfect and perfectly committed to us. He wants to share every moment of our lives, because he is simply that interested in us, like the oldest friend, the one we can always count on. That is how God is. The more deeply and fully we believe that, the easier and more natural it will be to live always in his presence.

HOW CAN I LEARN TO PRAISE GOD?

The desire to praise God, which is written on the human heart, is often obscured or deadened by the cares and worries of life in a fallen world. Praise is a kind of prayer, so understanding what distinguishes it may help you in your efforts to do it. We'll start there, and then point out some ready-made prayers of praise that can serve you as models and coaches.

The Essence of Praise

In prayer, we address God in five basic ways, which are easily remembered through the acronym of P.A.S.T.A.: Praise, Adoration, Sorrow for sin (as in contrition), Thanksgiving, and Asking (as in petition).

To praise someone, in general, is to speak well of his or her good qualities. Praising God, then, consists in acknowledging, recognizing, and admiring his infinite and incomparable excellence. Adoration, strictly speaking, moves a step beyond recognizing and admiring God's excellence; it involves an act of surrender to his will in response to that recognition. We can praise God's wisdom ("Your wisdom, Lord, is as vast as the ocean") and then, when we adore him, we submit to that wisdom ("I adore you, Lord, and put my life in your hands: Thy will be done"). Praise and adoration often flow into each other in practice.

Thanksgiving is a bit different from either praise or adoration. By giving thanks to God, we express our gratitude and indebtedness to the goodness and generosity with which he has treated us specifically. We praise God for being infinitely wise, but we thank him for his wise guidance to us personally: "Thank you, Lord, for leading me faithfully along the path of my vocation." Expressing sorrow for our sins and asking for good things from God are not prayers of praise per se. Yet, they do give glory to God in a similar way, because they indirectly acknowledge and show appreciation for both his mercy (otherwise we would not approach him for forgiveness) and his goodness (otherwise we would not approach him with our needs and desires).

The Value of Praise

Reflecting on these distinctions will lead you to a deeper appreciation of praise as the fundamental and primary form of prayer. Unless we perceive and acknowledge something of God's greatness, we will not be moved to adore him, thank him, or appeal to his mercy and generosity. If prayer is a "vital and personal relationship with the living and true God" (*CCC* 2558), then praise must be the very foundation of that relationship. We are not equals with God. We are completely dependent on him, infinitely lesser than him. And so, if our relationship with him is to be authentic (honest), the first gesture of our heart when we turn to God must be a gesture of humility. We must allow ourselves to be filled with wonder and awe at his majesty, and at his mind-boggling loving kindness as evidenced by the simple fact that he has created us (he didn't need to), has redeemed us (we didn't deserve it), and has continuously invited us to walk with him toward our everlasting home in his heavenly kingdom.

If in our busyness and suffering we neglect to gaze at God's greatness and praise him for it, our relationship with him will languish. We will stay infantile, overly and stiflingly absorbed in ourselves and our immediate needs. To grow in our friendship with God, we must stay rooted in true humility—like the tax collector, not the Pharisee (see Luke 18:9–14.) This is the reasoning behind starting our daily time of mental prayer with acts of faith, hope, and love; these are prayers of praise to God for his truth, power, and goodness. It is also the reason behind the frequent use of the Glory Be, another prayer of praise to the Blessed Trinity.

Your desire to praise God is already a prayer of praise. As long as you accept the simple fact that you will never be able to praise God fully, since he is infinite and we and our words and gestures are finite, I will offer some suggestions that may help you fulfill your desire to do so better.

Developing a Heart Full of Praise

First of all, join your own words and desires of praise to those of Christ. Jesus, as true man and true God, can praise the Father fully. When we unite our prayers to his, our imperfect and finite prayers are swept up into his infinite and perfect prayer. This is really what the Mass is all about. Read over the Eucharistic Prayers of the missal, and then, during Mass, really listen to the words of the priest and unite yourself to them. In this way, your praise will be magnified and elevated through its contact with Christ's own praise.

Something similar happens during adoration of the Blessed Sacrament. In the Sacrament, Jesus continues to offer himself to the Father for us; his incarnation, with all of his activities and mysteries, is somehow present in the Eucharist. When we kneel in adoration in his presence, our lives are linked to his life and lifted up, with him, to the Father. This is an expression and mode of praise.

Second, use prayers from the Bible and make them your own. The Our Father begins with praise and adoration and ends by covering every aspect of P.A.S.T.A. It really is the model prayer. If you haven't read the section in the *Catechism* on the Our Father (in Part IV), I highly recommend that you do so. You will discover dizzying depths of meaning in those few words, and they will become for you more powerful vehicles of praise.

But many other prayers of praise can be found in the Scriptures, and the Holy Spirit put them there precisely because he knew we would need help to express our admiration and awe (as well as our confusion and sorrow) when we address the Lord. Look for instance at the first part of Esther's prayer and Judith's prayer (in the books of Esther and Judith, respectively), and flip through the Psalms (for example, Psalms 19, 103, and 104). We have a library of inspired praise at our fingertips.

Third, if you like to write, you may want to compose some of your own psalms of praise, expressing in your own words your appreciation of those characteristics of God that most moved you. Even if you are not a writer, you may surprise yourself if you try this exercise. Each one of us has an individualized experience of God, and composing your own prayers of praise can help bring that experience into greater focus, thus giving great glory to the Lord. You also may find it useful to memorize a few hymns, songs, or poems that resonate in your heart, and use these as prayers of praise.

Fourth, use litanies. Many Christians don't understand the purpose of litanies, which seem like long lists of mechanically repetitive phrases. One of their purposes, however, is precisely to meet the need you expressed in your question. So often we just don't have adequate words to express what is in our hearts. And so, we place those inexpressible sentiments inside the words of a litany, trusting that the Holy Spirit will do the work of a good interpreter: "Likewise the Spirit helps us in our weakness; for we do not know how to pray as we ought, but the Spirit himself intercedes for us with sighs too deep for words" (Romans 8:26). I personally like the Litany of the Sacred Heart and the Litany of the Holy Name of Jesus.

Finally, don't be afraid of silence. Gazing with delight in your heart at God's beauty and magnificence is in itself a prayer of praise that gives God great pleasure and deepens your relationship with him. In these times, often simply repeating the name of the Lord, "Jesus," is praise enough. As Benedict XVI put it in a homily on July 4, 2010:

Let us not be afraid to be silent outside and inside ourselves, so that we are able not only to perceive God's voice, but also the voice of the person next to us, the voices of others.... We must be attentive, always keep our "interior eyes" open, the eyes of our heart. And if we learn how to know God in his infinite goodness, then we will be able to see, with wonder, in our lives—as the saints did—the signs of that God, who is always near to us, who is always good to us, who says: "Have faith in me!"

WHAT DOES IT MEAN TO HAVE A PERSONAL RELATIONSHIP WITH JESUS?

If you pray and go to Mass regularly, why do you do it? Why would you carve time out of your busy schedule to pray the Rosary and worship God? Most likely, your personal answer fits into one of the following three generic answers, and these answers will determine whether you move into a relationship with Jesus that is personal and intimate.

First, we can pray and worship out of routine. It's like punching a spiritual time clock. We've always prayed, always gone to Mass, ever since we were kids, and we feel a kind of comfortable inertia in continuing to do so. We have a vague sense that we ought to do such things, and we have a vague sense that if we fail to do them, we will feel guilty for some reason, and we don't want to add an uncomfortable guilty feeling to our already over-stressed emotional world. So we keep going through the motions of being a Catholic. Just as it would strike an American citizen as somehow incongruent not to celebrate the Fourth of July, it strikes a cultural Catholic as somehow incongruent not to engage in some basic spiritual practices. If you say your prayers just because doing so has become part of your internal comfort zone, you may have fallen into what theologians call spiritual routine.

When I was in eighth grade, I remember sleeping over at a friend's house. As we went down to the basement to go to bed, his parents were sitting on the couch watching television, the wife cuddling against the husband, who had his arm around her. They looked like a happy couple. Two months later they were divorced. I asked my friend how they could seem so happy together and then get divorced. My friend told me that they just kept up appearances for the kids' sake, but there was no love in it. That's falling into routine.

Second, we can pray and worship out of fear. This can be akin to superstition. We have the idea in our heads that if we stop going to Mass, praying the rosary, or making our morning offering, God will become angry, punish us, make our lives miserable, and maybe even send us to hell. In this case, our spiritual commitments (prayer and worship) are like paying taxes to a tyrant, or being extorted by a strongman: If we pay our dues, the Boss won't bother us.

In ancient pagan religions, proper worship depended on following formulas exactly. A priest had to offer an elaborate ceremony with perfect execution, or the god would not be pleased, and it would go to waste. During the ceremony, if the priest sneezed, for example, he would have to start all over again. In this religious vision, people are not children of a loving Father, but slaves of angry, fickle, and aloof deities.

Third, we can pray and worship out of conviction. The word *conviction* comes from the same word that gives us *convinced.* Religious conviction is an internal state of assurance with regard to religious truth. The primary reason convinced Christians pray and worship is because they sincerely believe that Jesus Christ is the Son of God, our Lord and Savior, Creator and Redeemer; they believe that he deserves their praise, and they need his grace.

If our spiritual life flows from conviction, then the actual activity we engage in during our times of prayer is conscious: We pay attention to the meaning of the words, we search the Scriptures for wisdom and guidance, we lift our hearts to God in thanksgiving and adoration, and we strive to conform how we live to what we discover in prayer—to what God wants for us (God's will). In this case, our faith actually connects our mind and heart to God during our prayer. We are not just going through motions, not just paying our dues; we are actually encountering the God who speaks to his beloved children through the revelation of Jesus Christ.

Conviction Makes It Personal

Praying and worshipping mainly out of conviction (as opposed to routine or fear) is what it means to have a personal relationship with Christ. On the one hand, we know that he knows us and is interested in our life ("No longer do I call you servants...I have called you friends.... You did not choose me, but I chose you and appointed you that you should go and bear fruit." (John 15:15–16). Or, as St. Paul put it, "I live by faith in the Son of God, who loved me and gave himself for me" (Galatians 2:20). And on the other hand, we put forth our own effort to follow his example and teaching, as a way to stay close to him. We accept his invitation to become a disciple, and we participate in his great project of building up the Church for the glory of God and the salvation of souls: "If you love me, you will keep my commandments" (John 14:15). Christianity is about knowing, loving, and following a person: Jesus Christ. The essence of our religion is a personal relationship of faith, hope, and love.

Heart to Heart

As Benedict XVI put it in his inaugural homily:

> The Church as a whole and all her Pastors, like Christ, must set out to lead people out of the desert, towards the place of life, towards friendship with the Son of God, towards the One who gives us life, and life in abundance.... There is nothing more beautiful than to be surprised by the Gospel, by the encounter with Christ. There is nothing more beautiful than to know Him and to speak to others of our friendship with Him.... If we let Christ into our lives, we lose nothing, nothing, absolutely

nothing of what makes life free, beautiful, and great. No! Only in this friendship are the doors of life opened wide. Only in this friendship is the great potential of human existence truly revealed. Only in this friendship do we experience beauty and liberation.[1]

Of course, we are all on our way to spiritual perfection, and so sometimes we fall into routine—at least, on the surface of our minds we can fall into routine; our conviction still exists, but it's submerged under distraction or anxiety. That prayer is still valuable, and still pleasing to God; the remote motivation is right on target. But the more we can keep our convictions fresh, strong, and vibrant, the better.

Likewise, I may find myself crawling out of bed on Sunday to get ready for Mass just because I know that missing Mass is a mortal sin, and I really don't want to go to hell. Some Christian faith and conviction is still present even in that slavish motivation. God can work with that. Yet the more we understand what the Mass really is, the more we will see obeying the precept to attend Mass as a joy, a relief, a mysterious encounter with eternity, and an opportunity to please God and build up his kingdom. When we pray and worship out of conviction, we connect better with Christ, and his grace has more room to work in our souls.

Having a personal relationship with Christ doesn't mean regularly having visions of him sitting on the easy chair in the living room or hearing him give us directions while we're looking for the right exit off the Interstate. Rather, it simply means gradually learning to live our Christianity more and more from heart to heart.

WHAT IS THE DIFFERENCE BETWEEN CONSOLATION AND DESOLATION?

Usually, these terms refer to the *felt presence* of God in our soul (consolation), or the absence of that feeling (desolation). By faith we know that God is always thinking of us, always with us, always interested in our lives, and always loving us with a personal, determined love. We *know* that by faith. But we don't always *feel* that in our emotional world. In fact, sometimes we can feel an intense and painful emptiness inside. We might feel absolutely no excitement or pleasure at the thought of spiritual things. Sometimes we can feel dry as a desert even when we are at prayer: Emotionally, we don't even want to keep praying. We are like children with their homework: They know it is good for them to do it, and they know they should do it, but they just don't feel like doing it.

This lack of the *felt presence* of God, this lack of emotional pleasure or resonance regarding God's will for us, is usually referred to by spiritual writers as *sensible desolation*. The contrary is *sensible consolation*.

If you are experiencing desolation, it can come from a variety of sources. Simply knowing what those sources are can help us reflect on one's personal situation and, usually, identify its source.

Our Own Fault

First, desolation can be caused by our own sin. We may be inordinately attached to something: some habit, some relationship, some hope, some fear, even some hobby or pastime that may not be evil in itself. Or perhaps we have committed some sin that we haven't confessed or repented of yet. Sooner or later, disordered attachments will interfere with our relationship with God. God loves us too much to let us idolize anything for long. If we are following him, when the time is right he will speak to our conscience about putting that disordered room in our soul back in order. During the struggle to decide whether or not to obey what he is asking of us, we can experience desolation, because as we dillydally, our hearts are divided. In this case, we are actually pushing God away, and the desolation is our own fault. This happens frequently in the early stages of the spiritual life, but it can return with a vengeance even after much growth, when certain sins attempt to reconquer the soul.

It can be hard to identify disordered attachments. If you are praying consistently (including at least an annual spiritual retreat), doing a daily examination of conscience, going to confession on a regular basis, receiving some kind of spiritual direction (or at least you have a friend or small group of friends to whom you make yourself spiritually accountable), and following the commandments of God and the Church, you should be able to recognize these disordered attachments when the Holy Spirit points them out to you. If you are not following these basic spiritual practices, your desolation may stem from this, and I would recommend renewing your commitment to the means for spiritual growth that all spiritual writers recommend.

Our Fallen Nature's Fault

Second, desolation can flow from advancing self-knowledge. As we grow in the spiritual life, God allows us to know ourselves better and better. We begin to see just how deep our self-centered tendencies really go. We become aware of how vulnerable we are to temptations of vanity, pride, and sensuality. We discover how helpless we really are when it comes to growth in holiness, without the constant aid of God's grace. This can create a disturbance in our relationship with God, because we no longer feel worthy of the great love he has for us. We truly love God. We truly want to follow him. But when we resist approaching him because we have discovered that we actually don't deserve to be loved so unconditionally, we begin to stumble. It's like the spouse who has been unfaithful and has difficulty accepting their spouse's forgiveness, or the mother who has aborted her child and simply can't seem to accept God's mercy. But in this stage of the spiritual life, the *specific* cause of the interior resistance is often less clear. Here again, we end up separating ourselves from God.

This hurdle has to be faced and overcome in order to become spiritually mature. You have probably already detected the real source of the spiritual reluctance that comes from this situation. It is a subtle form of pride. The enemy of our souls will often seize on this, stir it up, and try to exaggerate it. The truly humble soul responds to its own unworthiness with peace and joy, throwing itself into God's arms with total abandon, totally conscious of its absolute need for God's grace, and contentedly aware of God's delight in showing mercy to his needy children.

The deep interior resistance so many people experience when it comes to activating that kind of abandonment shows just how difficult developing the virtue of humility really is. It is the bedrock of the spiritual life, and digging foundations is never fun. But you can do it. Read the lives of the saints (especially St. Thérèse of Lisieux's *Story of a Soul* and St. Faustina's *Diary*). Read the Psalms. And get on your knees in front of the Eucharist, simply learning to trust more deeply in God's goodness by exercising whatever level of trust you can as you gaze at Our Lord, who has *chosen to be there for you, no matter what.*

The Doctor of Your Soul

Finally, desolation can flow from God's direct action on the soul. God can take away the consolation of his presence, without actually taking away his presence. This is a method he uses to purify the soul and to increase the soul's capacity for love. If you can keep following God's will in your life even when you are passing through a "valley of the shadow of death" (Psalm 23:4), you will emerge with a much more mature faith, a more vibrant hope, and a deeper love. These are the theological virtues that unite the soul to God—and union with God is what you were created for, and what God yearns for you to achieve and deepen.

So when he takes away interior consolation in this way, you can rest assured that his wisdom and goodness will permit you, when you've emerged from the darkness, to undergo greater consolations than you ever imagined, because your soul's capacity to experience God will have been increased by God directly. These periods of purification initiated by God are often called the "dark night." There are dark nights of the senses, of the spirit, of the intellect.... This is when God, the doctor of your soul, lays you on the spiritual operating table and takes direct action. Your job in this case is to trust and endure by continuing to seek and embrace God's will in your life (the commandments, the duties of your state in life, etc.). The recent book on Blessed Mother Teresa of Calcutta, *Come Be My Light: The Private Writings of the Saint of Calcutta,*[2] chronicles a truly amazing journey through this kind of darkness.

When all else fails, I recommend taking up the prayer Jesus taught us through St. Faustina and making it the constant refrain of your heart and mind throughout every season of your spiritual journey: "Jesus, I trust in you."

WHAT IS REDEMPTIVE SUFFERING— WHAT DOES IT MEAN TO "OFFER IT UP"?

If we are in the state of grace, our prayers, virtuous actions, and even our sufferings can become a source of merit. When we unite them to Christ (offer them up), they become pipelines of grace extending from the heart of Christ into our hearts and through us into the Church and the world around us. That said, we also must remember that the diameter of the pipeline is not fixed. It depends upon four factors, and growth in spiritual maturity depends to a great extent on the interior discipline required in living out these four factors.

First, there is the amount of sanctifying grace present in my soul. The more I am filled with grace, the more merit my prayers, virtuous actions, and sufferings will have when I offer them to God. The more grace I am infused with, the higher the wattage on the lamp of my soul. This is because grace is what makes us more like God, more united to him. A kind word from a stranger can be pleasant, but a kind word from someone dear to me is much more meaningful. The Christian who prays daily, receives the sacraments regularly, and makes an effort to practice all the Christian virtues, rooting out sinful tendencies and avoiding sin, is more united to God. They are in a better position to merit. As the Bible puts it, "The LORD is far from the wicked, / but he hears the prayer of the righteous" (Proverbs

15:29). And lest you think this is just an Old Testament anachronism, St. James makes the same point in the New Testament: "The prayer of a righteous man has great power in its effects" (James 5:16). What goes for prayer goes also for virtuous actions and sufferings.

Second, there is our union with Jesus. This is closely related to the first factor, but it is less formal and more relational. It's a question of being aware of our union with Christ. We are members of his mystical body, and so he is always with us. The more conscious we are of this union, the more meritorious all of our actions become. When we are working on a project with another person, the beneficial synergy happens more fully and dramatically if we are in constant contact with that person through the whole process. Our project as Christians is to build up Christ's kingdom in our hearts and in the world around us. If we try to do the work on our own and then check in with the Lord at the end of the day, that's good. But it's much better if we work side by side with him throughout every phase of the project. This is the spiritual discipline of living in the presence of God, and it turns even the most mundane tasks into meaningful encounters with God. If I am habitually living and working while aware of Christ's presence in my heart, then saying the words "Lord, I offer this up to you" resonates deeply in my soul, opening up a wider flow of God's grace (merit) through that offering. St. Paul encouraged the Christians of Colossae to practice this spiritual discipline: "Whatever you do, in word or deed, do everything in the name of the Lord Jesus, giving thanks to God the Father through him" (Colossians 3:17).

Third, there is our purity of intention. We can offer up our sufferings, using them to gain merit, for many different reasons: because we don't want to go to hell; because we want more glory in heaven; because we want our sufferings to win graces for others who are in need; because we want to show God that we love him no matter what, even if he permits suffering in our lives; because we want to conform our lives more perfectly to Christ. The same variety of reasons can be present in our prayers and virtuous actions. We can obey because we don't want to be punished, or because we recognize that the virtue of obedience is pleasing to God and glorifies his wisdom; we can exhaust ourselves to earn a decent living because we are afraid of being labeled a failure, or because we recognize that God has given us a mission to provide for a family and thereby be a mirror of the Father's goodness.

The default setting for our interior intention is usually self-centered. But with God's help and constant effort on our part, we can make it more and more mission-centered, kingdom-centered, Christ-centered. Of course, usually we have more than one intention—for example, we work for the satisfaction of a job well done but also to benefit the world around us and to make a living, and also to glorify God. Multiple intentions are natural and normal; human beings are complex creatures. But the more we can consciously renew our supernatural intention, stirring up the reasons for doing things that are based on the wisdom of our faith, the bigger pipeline of grace we can become. This factor applies even to the littlest things we do, as St. Paul makes clear: "So whether you eat or drink, or whatever you do, do all to the glory of God" (1 Corinthians 10:31).

Fourth, there is the factor of fervor. There can be twenty kids in a math class, and every single one of them can be working on an exercise. But not all of them will be putting their whole heart into it. There might be fifteen kids at baseball practice, but not all fifteen will be giving their all for the whole two hours. Just so, we can all say the words, "Lord, I offer this up to you," but we will not all say them with equal fervor; the more meaning we pour into them, the more merit we can acquire. When sufferings come our way, for example, we can accept them with different degrees of fervor: reluctance, patience, gratitude, joy.

As long as we accept them out of faith, we will merit—we will help increase the flow of grace in the Church. But if we accept them with a greater degree of faith ("Lord, you are giving me a chance to unite myself more closely to Christ on the cross; help me to share his love as I share his pain!"), there will also be a greater degree of merit. Jesus stressed this when he identified the most important commandment: "You must love the Lord your God with all your heart, and with all your soul, and with all your mind" (Matthew 22:37). He said *all.* The implication is that we can love with different degrees of totality.

Sanctifying grace, union with Jesus, purity of intention, and *fervor* are four factors that help determine the degree of merit that our prayers, virtuous actions, and sufferings (sacrifices) can win for ourselves, the Church, and the world around us. So there is much more to uniting our sufferings to Christ than simply saying the words, though that is the necessary catalyst.

I hope this hasn't discouraged you by giving the impression that the spiritual life is overly complicated. It really isn't. In fact, knowing that one simple action (a prayer, a headache, an act of service, an honest word, a chore) can either open up a trickle or a torrent of grace is a jewel of wisdom. It should fill us with optimism and enthusiasm. We don't have to convert nations or face lions in the Coliseum to do something glorious for God! Nor do we have to learn complex yoga techniques in order to develop spiritual maturity—we just have to dig deep into our soul before, during, and after our normal activities, and activate our faith so as to plug them into our Christian mission of building Christ's kingdom. (By the way, the easiest way to do that is to grow in the habit of praying "constantly"— see 1 Thessalonians 5:17. When we do that, the four factors kick in and intensify automatically.) This is less glamorous than becoming a martial arts expert, because it is largely interior and invisible (to everyone except you and God), and therefore requires more discipline. As St. Paul put it, we "walk by faith, not by sight" (2 Corinthians 5:7).

But the good news is, as always, that we are not alone. God, Mary, the angels and the saints are all very eager to help us, if we just give them the chance.

Chapter Two

Spiritual Formation

FROM A CHRISTIAN PERSPECTIVE, THE degree of fulfillment we experience here on earth is directly proportionate to the depth of our communion with God in Christ. And that communion depends upon using and developing our spiritual faculties properly.

The proper exercise of one's capacity for *self-awareness* involves discovering and assimilating *truth*—the truth about God, about the human family, about oneself, about the world. The proper exercise of one's capacity for *self-determination* involves choosing what is morally *good*—that which actually helps us to live out our vocation to image God here in the visible world.

By seeking and adhering to truth and goodness, we can attain spiritual maturity (the healthy development of our spiritual faculties), a necessary precondition for lasting happiness. In this chapter, we'll look at various obstacles that impede our progress in being formed spiritually, as well as the practical ways those obstacles can be overcome.

HOW CAN I LEARN TO TRUST GOD?

The need for trust is at the very core of the Christian journey. Sin separates us and distances us from God. All sin—our own personal sins as well as the sins of others, both of which damage our souls—traces its origin back to the Fall of Adam and Eve (that's why their sin is called "original sin"). What was the essence, the deepest core of their sin? We tend to think it was *disobedience*. Think again, though: disobedience was the trunk, but it grew out of an even deeper root. Here's how the *Catechism* puts it:

Man, tempted by the devil, let his *trust in his Creator die in his heart* and, abusing his freedom, disobeyed God's command. This is what man's first sin consisted of. All subsequent sin would be disobedience toward God and *lack of trust in his goodness.* (*CCC* 397, emphasis added)

Trust: The Heart of Holiness

Rehabilitating trust in God is every Christian's primary project for growth in holiness. Each of us has our own journey. Our experiences in life, good and bad, can damaged our capacity to trust in God in a personal, unique way. Our mission in life, our vocation, our way of knowing, loving, and serving God is also personal and unique. And so, the path each of us takes to rehabilitate our trust in God will have certain twists and turns, certain epiphanies and setbacks, that will be entirely our own. But, in the end, relearning to trust God is for each one of us the central, defining spiritual project.

How do you develop trust when you don't have much? How can you develop gratitude when you don't have humility? And how can you develop humility if you have a strong pattern of self-reliance?

Let me answer these questions with another question. Let's pretend you don't know how to play tennis, but you decide that you want to learn. How do you do it? How do you go from zero to beginner to intermediate to advanced? How do you develop the physical skills and coordination and muscle memory necessary for tennis when you have none of those things? The answer, I think you will agree, is fairly simple. You learn to play tennis by playing tennis.

Holy Tennis

Growth in virtue (trust, confidence in God, surrender, humility, and gratitude) is similar. Virtues are *moral habits,* just as skills are *physical habits.* They are developed under two conditions. First, it's necessary to have the raw material. Future tennis players have to have the normal use of all the major muscle groups (you can't play tennis without arms).

Future saints have to have the normal use of human nature: "heart, soul, mind, and strength" as our Lord put it in Luke 10:27. Virtues are not developed "once and for all." We can never check a virtue like trust off our to-do list. We grow in trust, little by little, by trusting. We grow in humility, little by little, by exercising self-denial. We grow in gratitude, little by little, by saying thank you, sincerely and intentionally, over and over again, especially when we don't feel like it. The sacraments nourish these efforts; prayer and spiritual reading inform and enlighten these efforts; the Holy Spirit—directly, through a spiritual director or mentor, through faith-based friendships, and through God's providence—will coach you.

St. John of the Cross put it succinctly when writing about the virtue of love (which is the core of every virtue, so it applies equally to trust, humility, gratitude): "Where there is no love, put love, and you will find love."[3]

As long as you are *patient,* even the tiniest effort to trust God will give God's grace a chance to touch your soul and strengthen the very trust that you are using. Remember, at baptism you received sanctifying grace and the gifts of the Holy Spirit, and at confirmation you received a strengthening of them. God is already at work in your life. He is drawing you closer to him. The journey will take your whole life, so don't think that you have to make yourself perfect before God can do anything with you. On the contrary! God is already working in and through your life! Your desire to know and follow him better is already a clear sign that you are growing!

Two Time-Tested Trust Workouts

On a practical level, the saints all agree on two spiritual exercises that *directly* strengthen our capacity to trust God.

First, meditate on Christ's passion. As we gaze on Christ "loving us to the end" (see John 13:1), our fears are quelled and we realize, gradually, that even though everyone else may have betrayed us and wounded us and lost their trustworthiness, Christ will never betray us. He is worthy of our trust. No matter what happens, he will keep on loving us. That's one of the core messages of the passion.

Second, focus on discovering and embracing God's will in the nitty-gritty of your daily life. We know what God's will is through his commandments, through the teachings of the Church, through the duties of our state in life, and through the circumstances of God's providence. Lord, what do you want me to do right now? That question, that prayer, is a powerful ally in your path of growing trust. Why? Because every time we accept and embrace and try to fulfill God's will, even with a fragile love and flimsy faith, we are actually exercising our trust in God. We are saying, "Okay Lord, I don't really understand this completely, but I know that you want me to do it, so here goes." That counts for simple tasks like washing the dishes. And it counts for more daunting tasks like talking about the faith or defending a Catholic position in a conversation at work. This is especially true when God's will contradicts our natural preferences. That's when we get to carry our own crosses, which is the privileged place for exercising, and therefore growing in, our trust in God.

HOW CAN I LEARN TO LOVE GOD?

If we were having an in-person conversation, my response to your question would be another question: "What do you mean by *love?*" It's a word that can be used in many ways. Let's start by reflecting together on that term.

Love as Emotion

Love can be an emotion. As an emotion, it consists of a feeling of attraction toward someone or something. Along with that feeling of attraction, we experience a desire to possess or be connected to the loved object. In this sense, we can talk about loving ice cream, or cats, or movies. This meaning is also linked to the experience of falling in love, which involves a powerful, sometimes almost overwhelming, feeling of attraction for another person. Often this feeling is immediate, mysterious, and irrational. That doesn't make it any less energizing, influential, or important.

Love as Virtue

The word *love* can also refer to *virtue*: the virtue of wanting another person to exist and flourish. This is what our Lord referred to when he commanded us to "love your neighbor as yourself" (Matthew 22:39). This is a decision to seek and promote the good of others, regardless of how you feel toward them. You may feel a strong emotional aversion to someone, but you can still love that person in this sense of the virtue—in fact, you are commanded to love the person in spite of contrary emotions. Another term used to describe this kind of Christian love, which considers only the need of the other, not one's own emotional attachment, is mercy (and sometimes charity).

The Church has taught from the first Christian centuries that the virtue of loving one's neighbor is central and critical to Christian living. Traditionally, the Church recommends the works of mercy as the normal channels for us to exercise this love. The *Catechism* summarizes it this way:

> The *works of mercy* are charitable actions by which we come to the aid of our neighbor in his spiritual and bodily necessities. Instructing, advising, consoling, comforting are spiritual works of mercy, as are forgiving and bearing wrongs patiently. The corporal works of mercy consist especially in feeding the hungry, sheltering the homeless, clothing the naked, visiting the sick and imprisoned, and burying the dead. (*CCC* 2447, emphasis in original)

As with every virtue, to grow in love requires exercising love. And so, a key way for us to grow in love is simply to exercise this virtue of love. We are to make a concerted effort to serve others, to seek and promote what is good for them, and to do so as Christ has done with us, with great patience, kindness, and selflessness (see 1 Corinthians 13).

Love as Supernatural Charity

This same word can be used in yet a third way: for *supernatural charity*. This refers to the love of God himself, the love the three persons of the Trinity have for each other, and the love God has for us. It also refers to the theological virtue that Christians receive at baptism and develop as they mature spiritually. It enables the Christian to love God with the very love of God—in other words, it enables us to enter into the circle of love that is the Trinity. We become part of God's own family through this supernatural gift of grace that shows itself forth in theological charity. But it also overflows: As we love God with his own Trinitarian love, we find ourselves loving others and even all things in God and for God.

This is the love that Christ referred to when he gave his New Commandment: "Love one another as I have loved you" (John 15:12). It's the love shown by the saints, like Blessed Teresa of Calcutta, whose love for her neighbor reached such a heroic degree. The connection between our loving God and our loving our neighbor was made explicitly by Christ in the Gospels. It would be a contradiction to say that we love God when we refuse to accept, serve, and appreciate our neighbors. After all, God loves all people, so if we really love him, we too will love all people. This love for God also shows itself in our obedience to God's will in our lives. Jesus was "obedient unto death...on a cross" out of his love for the Father and for us (Philippians 2:8). And so, obedience to God's will out of love for God is another means for growing in love—it exercises our love for God and therefore increases it.

To love God means to desire and pursue a greater communion with him at all times. This communion increases primarily through our reception of grace in the sacraments, and through our obedience to his will. It also increases through our efforts to imitate Christ in loving our neighbors (see 1 John 4:20). In this sense, loving God does not consist essentially in experiencing a strong emotional resonance when we think of God or enter into prayer. God may give us the emotional experience of love in our relationship with him (especially at the beginning of our spiritual journey—kind of like our spiritual honeymoon), but the essence is much deeper than emotion.

Growing in Love

As we grow spiritually, these three meanings of love come together. Our love for God begins to put order into our emotions, and we discover less contrast between our natural emotional preferences and the demands of virtue. Our love for God also begins to purify our minds and hearts, so we begin to see others as God sees them, and even their objective flaws and imperfections do not impede our appreciation of them. Likewise, as our love for God matures, we embrace his will with more and more emotional relish, even when his will contradicts our natural preferences.

But on the road to that maturity, these different loves can cause a lot of turbulence in the soul. We can simultaneously experience a profound emotional repugnance toward a person that we know we must serve with kindness. On the other hand, we can feel a powerful emotional attraction toward someone that we should not become emotionally involved with. In this case, the virtue of love will enable us to keep a respectful emotional distance. Sometimes it will take every ounce of our strength to resist a temptation against obedience to God's will. The spiritual life really is a battle.

Let us all continue to "walk by faith, not by sight" (2 Corinthians 5:7) as we strive to live a deeper love for God and neighbor. And in his wisdom, God will surely harmonize in our souls the emotion and the virtue of love, so that his joy may be in us, and our joy may be made full (see John 15:11).

HOW CAN I BE JOYFUL WHEN LIFE SEEMS HOPELESS?

First of all, none of us are alone in our sufferings. And the answer is not just putting on a happy face. Mature Christians are not Pollyannas. We don't pretend that life in this fallen world is supposed to be hunky-dory. There is a reason that the Church requires every public place of worship to prominently display a crucifix over the altar: Our journey home (to heaven) is a long and arduous journey, and during certain seasons of life, it can be really difficult. But Jesus tells us: "In the world you have tribulation; but be of good cheer, I have overcome the world" (John 16:33).

Basic Joy and Basic Hope

Joy is the experience of delight that comes from possession of something good. The delight is deeper and longer lasting the more profound the something good is. I experience joy when I eat a brownie, because it tastes good. But the taste goes away when the brownie goes away—a very passing joy. I experience joy when I win an Olympic gold medal, and that joy will last my whole life long, recurring whenever I think about it or hold the medal in my hands, because the victory was the result of a herculean effort, extended over a very long period of time.

Hope is the anticipation of joy, or embryonic joy. When the game is coming to a close and it looks like we are going to win, we are full of hope; we are experiencing, in a sense, joy in advance. Then, when the final whistle blows and the scoreboard shows us on top, hope blossoms into full-fledged joy, because the good thing, the victory, is finally ours.

A Key for Spiritual Maturity

One of the greatest challenges in the spiritual life is learning to live true Christian joy and hope. We live on earth, in this fallen world. And we have a fallen human nature. As a result, we have a default setting, so to speak, that makes us seek our happiness in the good things of this world. This could be sensual pleasure, popularity, our achievements—all extremely superficial goods. But we can also seek our happiness in authentic goods:

a healthy marriage and family, a good job that allows me to help build a better world, or a simple, balanced lifestyle that brings peace to me and those around me. Because this is our default setting, we have a strong tendency to experience deep frustration when these worldly goods let us down. We tend to think that we just need to make some kind of adjustment, and then happiness will be ours.

But there is a fundamental problem with this default setting: It is wrong. The goods of this world, whether superficial or profound, will never, *can* never, provide the deep, lasting joy that our hearts yearn for, that we were made for. Why? Here is the *Catechism's* answer (27):

> The desire for God is written in the human heart, because man is created by God and for God; and God never ceases to draw man to himself. Only in God will he find the truth and happiness he never stops searching for. (*CCC* 27)

Spiritual maturity, therefore, consists largely in learning to appreciate the goods of this world in a relative manner, as means to an end. It means learning to desire God more and more—to "love the Lord your God with all your heart, and with all your soul, and with all your mind, and with all your strength" (Mark 12:30).

Christian Joy

From this perspective, we can begin approaching what Christian joy and hope really means. Joy arises from our paying special attention to the fact that Jesus Christ came to earth two thousand years ago to conquer the powers of darkness and open the gates of heaven. He came to forgive us our sins, to heal us, to forge a path to everlasting life for us. This is an objective reality—an eternal good that we already possess through faith. But we need to remind ourselves of this good, this truth. We need to focus our attention on it, understand it, savor it, explore it, and let it fill our hearts. Only then will the deep joy Christ promises begin to stir in our hearts, a joy that no one can take from us, because no one can undo what Christ has done—the gates of heaven remain open!

Christian Hope

Not only has Jesus come and conquered evil, reversing original sin and opening to us the gates of heaven, but he has also promised—truly promised—that he will come again. And at his second coming, he will put an end to all injustice, sin, evil, and suffering: He will finish the story of salvation that was definitively begun with his first coming. We know that as long as we keep our friendship with him alive, we are guaranteed a share in that final victory, a place in the everlasting kingdom:

> In my Father's house are many rooms; if it were not so, would I have told you that I go to prepare a place for you? And when I go to prepare a place for you, I will come again and will take you to myself, that where I am you may be also. (John 14:2–3)

We can count on that. No matter how horrible our sufferings here on earth may be, Jesus has promised us the fulfillment of all desire, if only we persevere in our friendship with him. This is true Christian hope; this is a reason for hope that nothing can change or take away.

A Way Forward

The painful, exhausting tribulations God sometimes permits us to experience are, from a spiritual perspective, a golden opportunity. It helps us realize how passing, how fragile, how undependable even the good things of this world really are. The Holy Spirit invites us, as we continue forward with our share of Christ's cross weighing heavily on our shoulders, to lift our gaze to the light of Christ, the North Star leading us through this valley of tears toward our everlasting home. This is the perfect time for us to exercise true Christian hope and tap into deeper, sturdier Christian joy. Challenging times offer each of us a chance to go to an entirely new level in our Christian maturity.

How can we do that? It requires devoting more time to prayer and spiritual reading—especially about our fellow Christians who have also had to pass through dark and painful seasons in their journey home. And always remember, we are not alone. I'll finish with another quotation from our Lord: "Let not your hearts be troubled; believe in God, believe also in me" (John 14:1).

WHAT IS SPIRITUAL READING?

If daily meditation is like the bread and butter of your spiritual diet, spiritual reading is your multivitamin supplement. Spiritual reading explains some aspect of Catholic truth in an attractive, enriching way. Its function is to help reinforce and deepen our Christian view of ourselves and the world around us. In previous eras, popular culture itself was imbued with the Christian worldview, so even popular books and dramas reinforced the Christian value system. But now that is not the case. Instead, our minds are flooded every day by messages (advertisements, films, TV shows, news, music) that directly contradict the Christian worldview. That has an effect on how we think and what we value. In fact, this is one of the reasons the Church is suffering so much from so-called cafeteria Catholics. They get their Catholic information from secular sources (*The New York Times*, *Newsweek*, and so on), and so they simply can't understand why the Church would ever be against such popular and seemingly reasonable propositions like artificial contraception, artificial reproduction, and gay marriage. Because of this ongoing flood of secular ideals, we have to consciously nourish our minds with authentic Christian teaching in order to avoid being poisoned. That's what spiritual reading can do.

Spiritual reading is either instructive or refreshing. It either informs our minds so that we learn to think and understand more and more in harmony with divine revelation, or it refreshes what we already know and have learned by making it shine out more clearly once again. In either case, it counteracts the seductive, secularizing messages that saturate our cultural atmosphere. This is why spiritual reading is such an important spiritual discipline. It plants seeds of Christian truth in your mind, and they grow and germinate in your subconscious as you go about your daily business. These seeds often flower during your daily prayer and meditation; in fact, spiritual reading frequently provides topics, ideas, or insights that are excellent material for Christian meditation.

Getting Practical

Spiritual reading differs from regular reading not only in the content, but also in the method. You don't need to spend a lot of time doing spiritual reading; fifteen minutes a day is fine. And you don't need to read fast. The idea is simply to taste, chew on, and swallow some healthy Catholic concepts every day. The difference between spiritual reading and meditation is the end result. The goal of your meditation is to converse with the Lord about what matters to him and what matters to you. The reflection and consideration that forms part of your meditation is meant to spur that conversation in your heart. The goal of spiritual reading is to inform your mind; it doesn't finish with a prayerful conversation (though that can sometimes pop up spontaneously).

However, if you're not a reader, or if you think you don't have time, you can get creative. Good Catholic novels (novels imbued with a Catholic worldview, where characters exemplify Christian virtue in a realistic but inspiring way) can serve as a kind of spiritual reading. Listening to recordings of spiritual talks, homilies, or conferences (or books on tape, or good Catholic podcasts) while you drive or exercise can also do the trick.

The point here is that we all need to be always growing in our knowledge of the faith, because if we are not growing, we're withering.

HOW CAN I FIND COMFORT IN GOD WHEN I FEEL SO UNWORTHY?

First, make sure you cement into the very foundation of your understanding of the universe one extremely important truth that God has revealed to us so frequently and so forcibly that he has removed any room for doubt: "But God shows his love for us in that while we were yet sinners Christ died for us" (Romans 5:8). I would highly recommend that you memorize that verse of inspired Scripture and repeat it to yourself, using it as a prayer, throughout the day. God's love for his—his personal, all-knowing, passionate, tender, and determined love for each one of us—does not depend on our being worthy of it, being perfect, being selfless, being a model Christian. On the contrary, it is only as we continue discovering God's love for us that we open our hearts to be touched by his transforming grace so that we can actually love him in return and begin to experience life as he calls us to live it: selflessly, generously, joyfully, humbly. Our journey through this Valley of Tears that we call earth is not primarily about what we can do for God, but about what God has done (and still wants to do for us): "In this is love, not that we loved God but that he loved us and sent his Son to be the expiation for our sins" (1 John 4:10). Keep reminding yourself of this, over and over again. Make it the theme of your daily prayer. Ask God to convince you of this more and more every day.

From that perspective, I think you can answer your own question. How best to please God, even though you know that you are unworthy? Throw yourself into his arms. Dive into his mercy. Trust him when he tells you that he loves you just as you are, and maybe even more because you are so much in need of his grace. Remember the parable of the Good Shepherd, who left the ninety-nine sheep who were in good shape in order to go after the one sheep that was lost and in need. And he rejoiced when he found it. Your mere desire to follow God, to know him and love him better, gives him immense pleasure. Every time you turn back to him after a fall or a failure, you fill his heart with joy. He longs not for our self-perfection, but for our presence, our friendship, our desire to walk with him. This is what pleases him.

You may be confusing God being pleased with his being satisfied. God loves us so much that he is never satisfied. He knows we can grow, and so, like a good coach who really cares about his players, he never gets tired of demanding more from us and inviting us to give more. He loves us too much to let us vegetate in our personal comfort zone, spiritually speaking. But even though he is hard to satisfy, he is extremely easy to please. The slightest effort delights him! He knows better than we do how hard it is for us to live a truly spiritual, truly Christlike life. He is like a dad witnessing his little baby taking her first steps. The steps are clumsy, jerky, and unsteady. But how the dad rejoices over them!

Reality Check

Okay, now for a hard truth. Whenever you get drawn into a personal pity party and find yourself discouraged or tense or preoccupied about your own weakness and spiritual neediness (selfishness), you are actually falling into dangerous territory. Discouragement is not something that comes from the Holy Spirit—not ever. Discouragement is a very subtle form of spiritual pride, which is one of the seven capital sins. Discouragement, when we give into it and revel in it instead of turning it immediately into a prayer and throwing ourselves into God's loving arms, says to God: "O Lord, look at how evil I am; I am so selfish that not even you can love me or help me."

What a nasty trick of the devil that thought is! Oh, how it hurts our Lord when we say that to him! His mercy, his love, his goodness, his power—they are immensely greater than our misery! Our Lord revealed to St. Margaret Mary that, even if all the sins of the world were on her soul, compared to his burning love for her, they would be like a drop of water thrown into a blazing furnace. So, whenever you feel like turning in on yourself and being drawn into the pit of self-deprecation, simply make an act of humility and then turn your attention back to whatever it is God wants you to be doing at that moment, even if it's something simple or routine. "Lord, you know what a mess I am, but you love me. Give me the strength to forget about myself and do what you want me to do. I am in your hands, and they are Very Good Hands."

You might choose to take for a personal motto what St. Paul said about this very struggle, following his example of rejoicing in weaknesses because they force you to depend more and more on God, which is what it's all about: "I am content with weaknesses, insults, hardships, persecutions, and calamities; for when I am weak, then I am strong" (2 Corinthians 12:10).

HOW CAN I REGAIN MY PASSION FOR SPIRITUAL THINGS?

The spiritual life has two main sectors. The first sector is weeding out self-centered attitudes and behaviors. For instance, maybe we have been productive before, but we were doing it out of self-centered motives. Gradually we see the value in slowing down so the Lord can realign our hearts. An increase of time spent in prayer, spiritual reading, and other faith-centered activities creates some space for God to give us a more Christ-centered vision of ourselves, of God, and of the world. With Christ's help, we pull up a lot of weeds that were choking the garden patch of our soul. But just like the parable in the Gospels, where a man sweeps out his house and gets rid of all the devils, only to have seven more devils find it later on and move back in (see Luke 11), we all have tendencies to revert to self-centeredness if we only stay focused on that first sector. Besides, we also get bored.

The passage in Mark 3 where Jesus calls his twelve apostles is the model passage for the call every one of us receives from Christ, in a unique and personal way. But the essential structure of the call is the same for each. It has two parts. Jesus sets aside his chosen ones "to be with him, and to be sent out to preach and have authority to cast out demons" (Mark 3:14–15). This is the second main sector. We have responded to Christ's call to "be with him," to develop a life of prayer, to get to know his teaching, to spend time in his presence. Now it is time for us to take up the baton of our mission as his ambassadors in this world. He wants to send us out as his witnesses, his representatives, his soldiers, to spread the light of his truth and to roll back the forces of evil.

Where does he want you to go? Start close to home. Your first mission field is your immediate sphere of influence: family, parish, work, friends. How can you serve those people better? How you can place your gifts and talents at their service? How can you better mirror God's goodness to them and help them discover God's love—or, if they have discovered it already, how can you encourage and help them to live more and more in accordance with it? You may also have an opportunity to bear witness in a wider scope, depending on the possibilities God's providence has given you.

What does he want you to do? You spread Christ's light in three ways:

1. First, your way of being. The poise, elegance, simplicity, kindness, balance, responsibility, and humble charm with which you strive to do all your normal activities (chores, conversations, tasks) can, with God's help, send forth the sweet "aroma of Christ" (2 Corinthians 2:15).

2. Second, your words. Words are so powerful! We should always speak so as to help shed light, encourage, and bring joy, avoiding all unnecessary criticism, along with gossip, detraction, and calumny. "Let no evil talk come out of your mouth, but only such as is good for edifying, as fits the occasion, that it may impart grace to those who hear" (Ephesians 4:29). Growth in this area will boost your entire spiritual life and always give you more to shoot for, more ways to show and grow your love for God: "For we all make many mistakes, and if any one makes no mistakes in what he says he is a perfect man, able to bridle the whole body also" (James 3:2).

3. Third, your works. As Christians, not a day should go by without our taking the initiative to serve someone in need, whether the need is physical, emotional, or spiritual. We are members of the Body of Christ—we

are his hands and feet in this world. (A wise guide for this aspect of our mission in life is the traditional "works of mercy," which you can find listed in the *Catechism*, 2447.) You may also experience a strong desire in your heart—which could be a call from God—to get involved in a specific ministry or apostolate. More and more often now, lay men and women are being moved by the Holy Spirit to take the initiative in the New Evangelization and put their talents and experiences directly at the service of the Church's evangelizing mission.

In short, we are each like St. Paul. God has given us a vision of the light, and it has changed the direction of our interior lives. Each of us needs to pray what St. Paul prayed, getting ready for a new adventure: "What shall I do, Lord?" (Acts 22:10). As we begin to dedicate energy and time to developing this second sector—sowing new plants in the garden of our souls, not just pulling out the weeds—we will find once again the focus and the enthusiasm that seems to be missing. It is in loving that the fire of our hearts will be rekindled. And furthermore, our interior life, our "being with Christ" will also be affected. We will find that we experience more intensely our need for God's grace. We will develop a more fervent desire to encounter Christ and know him better. We will find that we have more—and more, and more, and more —to learn from and say to the Lord.

HOW CAN I STOP BEING SO IMPATIENT?

You will not like the answer to this question, but I will try to answer it anyway. There are two things you may be doing wrong—or you may be doing both of them.

First, you may be chopping off the visible stems of this weed of impatience in the garden of your soul, without digging up the roots. We all have a unique combination of selfish tendencies, and they express themselves in a unique combination of manifestations. (Think of a big weed with a lot of stems and branches.) When you're weeding a garden, you know that if you don't pull the root out, the weed will just grow right up again.

Impatience is one of the many offspring of the capital sin of pride, which is a disordered attachment to one's own excellence. We get impatient because deep down we have a strong tendency to think we are so smart, sharp, and gifted that we should be able to manage ourselves and our circumstances with perfect elegance. Therefore, we will never be able to overcome our impatient patterns of behavior simply by ordering ourselves to become more patient. Here and there, we might have tiny flashes of patience if we follow that strategy, but that's it. What is really need required is growing in the virtue of humility. Humility strikes impatience where it is rooted.

How do you grow in humility? Ask for the grace, first of all, every day. Second, continue your determined commitment to mental prayer, meditating on the life and words of Jesus, who is the perfect model of humility. Third, increase your conscientious use of the sacraments of confession and Communion. Finally, never let a day go by without making at least one small, hidden act of self-denial—such as purposely skipping a second helping of something you like, purposely not turning on the radio for the first five minutes of your commute, purposely not responding to someone who unfairly criticizes you.

Great Expectations

In the second place, your expectations may be wrong. Growth in any virtue does not follow a Hollywood-type schedule. In Hollywood, you can go from chump to champion in just two hours, like Peter Parker or Rocky Balboa. In real life, growth in holiness and virtue takes a long time and happens gradually. This is why Jesus always used parables involving seeds and growing things. If we sit and watch a seed grow, nothing seems to happen. But in fact, a lot is happening, if the parameters for growth (soil, water, sunlight) are present. In our spiritual lives, we too often want to see the fully matured fruit right now. Well, the fully matured fruit will not be seen this side of eternity. As the book of Job puts it: "Has not man a hard service upon earth, and are not his days like the days of a hireling?" (Job 7:1).

Frustration is almost always a function of expectations. If you have been working seriously on becoming a more patient person, following the example of Christ more closely, I can guarantee that you are more patient today than you were five years ago. So don't let the devil trick you into being frustrated with gradually becoming more and more patient, just because you aren't perfect yet. Instead, every time you fall, just brush yourself off, look up to heaven, and say, "You see what a pile of dust and ashes I am, Lord? Thanks for putting up with me. I know you'll never give up on me; help me never to give up on you."

HOW CAN I VIEW GOD AS A LOVING FATHER?

I'd like to begin my answer with a quotation from the *Catechism* that I have often reflected on:

> By calling God "Father," the language of faith indicates two main things: that God is the *first origin of everything and transcendent authority;* and that he is at the same time *goodness and loving care* for all his children. God's parental tenderness can also be expressed by the image of *motherhood,* which emphasizes God's *immanence,* the *intimacy* between Creator and creature. The language of faith thus draws on the human experience of parents, who are in a way the first representatives of God for man. But this experience also tells us that *human parents are fallible and can disfigure* the face of fatherhood and motherhood. We ought therefore to recall that God transcends the human distinction between the sexes. He is neither man nor woman: he is God. He also transcends human fatherhood and motherhood, although he is their origin and *standard:* no one is father as God is Father. (*CCC* 239, emphasis added)

In a sense, we have a built-in idea of what fatherhood ought to be. This instinct enables us to recognize the shortcomings of our own parents even before we learn explicitly about the Bible and God's self-revelation. My initial suggestion to someone who knows God but has experienced a less-than-ideal father is this: Consciously make acts of faith, hope, and love. We know that God's goodness is immense, unlimited, and uncontaminated by any self-centeredness or brokenness. We also know that he knows and loves us personally. These are simply tenets of our Catholic faith that we have received through the grace of baptism. This knowledge can grow in intensity and spread from one's mind into one's heart, will, and even emotions, if one exercises it. One way of exercising it is through the vocal prayers traditionally called acts of faith, hope, and love. These are short prayers we say in order to praise God for his goodness and reaffirm our loyalty to him. They can be said in the morning, at night, or even in little snippets of time throughout the day. Saying prayers like these, and really meaning them, exercises our confidence in God, and therefore strengthens it.

We can compose our own acts of faith, hope, and love, using words that resonate with our own experience of God, and with the yearning in our heart to cling to him more closely, more freely (that yearning is from the Holy Spirit). We can also use prayers composed by others. Below is a morning prayer we use in my congregation, with some comments in parentheses that show how these prayers can exercise our confidence in God:

PRAYER TO THE FATHER

Holy Father, it pleased you to create and adopt me so that I would love and invoke you with total trust, as your child.

(This places us in God's strong but gentle embrace. Our life comes from him; it is a gift, a personal gift, that implies a desire on his part for our presence, friendship, confidence. It all starts with him, with his immense goodness, the origin of all things.)

I bless you for the love you have shown me by choosing me in Christ, before the world was made, to be holy and perfect in your sight.

(This affirms our assurance that God has a plan for our lives. We are not just an accident; we are not lonely wanderers trying to make the best of a meaningless existence; Christ is a savior who involves us in a wonderful and meaningful story, the story of salvation.)

You know my frailty, and how much I need your grace to fulfill your holy will; so, Father, in your great love, grant me your grace in accordance with my needs.

(This invokes God the Father's ongoing care for us. He is interested in everything that happens to us and around us. He is involved in our lives. Our sins and weaknesses only increase his solicitude for us and his desire to come to our aid. He will never abandon us.)

Increase in my heart the burning zeal that will drive me tirelessly to bring everyone to share in the eternal life that consists in knowing and loving you, the only true God, and the one you sent, Jesus Christ.

(Here we ask God to give us the desires, courage, and wisdom we need to fulfill our life's mission. Again, God is on our side! He cares about us as the very best of Fathers!)

Grant me, holy Father, the fortitude I need to shun all sin and imperfection, and do not let me fall into the traps or give in to the temptations that the evil spirit sets for me today.

(God is also our protector. We invoke this protection and count on it, and it gives us confidence in the midst of life's struggles and the spiritual battles we face.)

Christ: The Revelation of God's Goodness

In addition to making acts of faith, hope, and love, the real shortcut to experiencing more and more deeply the strengthening goodness of God's Fatherhood consists in focusing on his Son. Jesus came to reveal to us the real nature of God, to show us God's face after original sin had blinded us and distorted our perception of our Creator and Lord: "The Word became flesh *so that thus we might know God's love*" (*CCC* 458; emphasis in original).

There is no better way to grow in a heartfelt knowledge and experience of God's goodness, of his infinitely tender and attentive love, then by delving into the "unsearchable riches of Christ" (Ephesians 3:8). The best way to do this is to make mental prayer a daily staple of your spiritual life, and to use as the subject of your prayer the four Gospels, or worthy commentaries on those Gospels. Spiritual reading is another excellent tool for growing in this knowledge.

Of course, contemplating God's wonders in creation, admiring his marvels in the lives of the saints, and enjoying the many small pleasures that God sends us each day (from sunsets to songs to chocolate) are all avenues to the same destination—these, too, are manifestations of God's goodness, of the Father's love.

A final word about this spiritual quest: Be patient. The need to rebuild our trust in God is a central need of every human heart. It is the core of the spiritual life, the only path to spiritual maturity and holiness. For this very reason, rehabilitating trust in God is a long process. But that's okay. Traveling this path is what God wants us to do, and it is in the traveling that we grow, and discover, and gradually experience more and more of the "peace of God, which passes all understanding" (Philippians 4:7)—a peace which alone will allow us find the fulfillment God has in store for us.

HOW DO I KNOW WHETHER I AM READY
FOR SPIRITUAL DIRECTION?

The first thing you need to know is that God is already hard at work in your soul. The mere fact that you are mulling this question over is proof of it. Imagine how pleased our Lord is as he sees you wanting to come closer to him and wondering about whether spiritual direction is a good next step. So many of his children never think of him at all, and you are thinking about new ways to know, love, and follow him better! This is clear evidence that the Holy Spirit is guiding you. And if he has been guiding you thus far, he will continue to do so. Be sure he will keep leading you on.

The easiest way for you to see if you are ready for spiritual direction is to try it. For example, you could go on a retreat (preferably a spiritual exercises retreat) and meet with a spiritual director during the retreat. See how it goes; see what it feels like; see if it helps you. Or, you could simply ask for a one-time meeting with a spiritual director to talk about what you are doing and what more you could be doing to grow spiritually. Having an initial experience will help you discern if God is offering you this means of growth. You can do this without making a long-term commitment.

But in general, I would offer two other observations. First, spiritual direction is not just for the elite. Every Christian can benefit from this kind of guidance, as long as they are sincere about trying to know, love, and follow Jesus more closely. You may have the impression that spiritual direction is only for spiritual marines. Not true. As a general principle, I would say that spiritual direction is the right thing for everyone all the time.

Second, you may be overestimating the role of spiritual direction. You don't graduate from confession to spiritual direction, for example. The sacraments, moral virtue, and prayer remain the irreplaceable staples of our spiritual diets. Spiritual direction merely helps us make better use of those means of growth that God has given us. It helps us create more space for the Holy Spirit to work in and through us. It is like a catalyst for improvement in the other, more central relationships and activities of life in a fallen world. Getting spiritual direction doesn't involve leaving any of those things behind.

Spiritual Direction in Scripture and Church Tradition
Do you remember when St. Paul had his encounter with the Lord on the road to Damascus? He asked the Lord what he was supposed to do, and

the Lord answered, "Rise, and go into Damascus, and there you will be told all that is appointed for you to do" (Acts 22:10).

Paul's question, "What shall I do, Lord?" is one of the most beautiful prayers in Scripture. These are words we can repeat in our hearts all day long, every day, as we travel the journey of faith. But Jesus's answer is rather puzzling. Jesus tells him to go into the city and wait for someone to come and tell him what to do. Why didn't Jesus just tell him right then? Why didn't Jesus give him another vision with a full list of instructions? We know from the rest of the scriptural narrative that God sent a Christian named Ananias to meet Paul, explain the Gospel to him, heal his blindness, and baptize him. Jesus didn't do all the work himself; he freely chose to work through others, to give his guidance through other human beings.

Then there was the remarkable encounter between the Ethiopian eunuch and the deacon Philip in Acts chapter 8. The eunuch had been on a pilgrimage to Jerusalem, even though he wasn't Jewish. He was a high-ranking official (chief treasurer, in fact) in Ethiopia's royal court. His pilgrimage was over, and he was on his way back south to his home country. Suddenly Philip was ordered by the Holy Spirit to catch up to the eunuch's chariot. When he did, he heard the eunuch reading the Jewish prophecies from Isaiah about the Messiah. Philip asked the man if he understood what he was reading, and the man answered, wisely, "How can I, unless someone guides me?" Why did the Holy Spirit send Philip to help this searching man find what he was looking for? Why didn't the Holy Spirit just give him the answer directly?

We could go on and on with similar examples from both the Old and New Testaments. Joshua was spiritually tutored by Moses, Elisha by Elijah, David by Nathan, Paul by Barnabas, Timothy by Paul, Mark by Peter…God's normal mode of operation is to guide and enlighten us by a combination of direct and indirect action; he stirs our souls and open our minds and gives us insights, but he helps us make sense out of them through the assistance of our fellow travelers, especially those he has called and gifted to make that a primary apostolate.

During the fourth century, at the beginning of the monastic movement, the institution of spiritual direction became more formalized. Young monks would receive instruction from older and more experienced monks as they pursued their vocation. This practice spread throughout Christendom quickly and even lay men and women eventually began to receive spiritual guidance from their confessors. In the years after the Protestant Reformation, the Jesuit order helped bring structure to the practice and took on spiritual direction as one of their major apostolates. Subsequently, both older and more recently formed orders have done the same. In the Church's new ecclesial movements, lay men and women are also being trained in the art of spiritual direction, so that it is more common to see laypeople not only receiving but also giving regular spiritual guidance.

Why does God choose to work in this way, both directly and also indirectly, through human instruments? Certainly we cannot fathom completely all of his reasons, but one of them is clear: God respects the human nature that he has given us. Because of that human nature, we are both material and spiritual beings, simultaneously matter and spirit. If God were to deal with us only through direct spiritual contact, he would be treating us like angels. But we are not angels. And so, to save us, he came up with the Incarnation—reaching out to us by becoming one of us. And he invented the Church, a real institution with a hierarchical structure and sacraments that transmit grace—a spiritual reality—through matter and material elements (messy and noisy matter, too—as anyone who has been up close at a baptism can attest!).

This combination of direct and indirect action on God's part is particularly clear in the case of the mystics. Jesus spoke directly to their souls, in an ongoing way, but they suffered immensely as they tried to discern how to respond to Jesus until he gave them a specially anointed spiritual director or confessor. *The Diary of St. Faustina* beautifully chronicles this kind of painful and confusing journey. How is it that he speaks to individuals directly, but they can't find peace and confidence until he gives them a human guide as well? That's our nature. God made it, God understands it, and God loves it. Blessed be God!

HOW CAN I CHOOSE THE RIGHT SPIRITUAL DIRECTOR?

First of all, remember that spiritual direction is a means, not an end. It is not meant to be the only source of input for your spiritual life or your only source of guidance. The Holy Spirit will continue to be your primary director. Your prayer, your spiritual reading, your participation in the sacraments, your personal reflection, your efforts to love your neighbor and fulfill God's will in your life—all these are still major channels of God's grace for you. You can still listen to God's voice through these channels, find his light there, and move toward greater intimacy with him.

Sometimes we make the mistake of thinking that our spiritual director is supposed to be in charge of our spiritual growth. While spiritual direction is a valuable, and perhaps necessary, element in the pursuit of spiritual maturity, each one of us is still in charge of our own lives; even God himself will never seize our freedom, and neither should a spiritual director (even though sometimes we feel like it would be a lot easier if he or she did!). God wants us to make use of spiritual direction, but he doesn't want our spiritual directors to replace our own freedom and creativity. Our friendship with Christ is still *our* friendship with Christ.

Patience Matters

Second, I would encourage you to be patient. Remember, the main protagonist in the spiritual direction relationship is actually the Holy Spirit. So, if you are doing your part to prepare and communicate, the Holy Spirit will be sure to act through the instrument of spiritual direction even if your director is a bit clumsy. God can handle that. The mere fact of communicating our spiritual experiences to a director exercises a number of key virtues—like faith, humility, and prudence—and sometimes that's all the Holy Spirit needs to keep us moving along the path of spiritual progress, regardless of the specific advice that a particular director may or may not offer.

Suggesting vs. Controlling

Third, you should feel completely free to make suggestions to your spiritual director about the structure of your conversations and the topics to be covered. Making suggestions is not the same as controlling. You can phrase your suggestions in a completely noncontrolling way. For example, "Father, thank you for our conversation—your comment about X was very helpful for me. After we talked, I was reflecting, and I think it would help me next time if we maybe start with a prayer. Would that be okay? And then, to help me stay focused, I would like to make sure that even if a lot of subjects come up, we talk specifically about my prayer life, my apostolate, and my constant battle with discouragement. Do you think it would be okay to keep those three topics on our 'list' every time we connect by phone? I will be sure to update you on what I am experiencing in those areas in my e-mail updates every couple weeks." This way, you can make suggestions that will be helpful for you, and they will not be threatening to your director. Taking the initiative in this way is not contrary to your to desire to have your director to direct you. Your director will surely give you specific recommendations as you continue developing your relationship and he continues to get to know you.

Looking Elsewhere

Fourth, what should you do if after a period of months you feel like no progress is being made? There is no obligation to continue receiving spiritual direction from someone whose direction is not helping you. But I wouldn't rush to a decision here. You will experience awkwardness, and so will your director, at the beginning—especially if you are attempting to receive spiritual direction from a distance. But this awkwardness should diminish gradually. If a number of months pass and it doesn't, then you should feel free to graciously conclude that the long-distance direction is not working. In that case, you could ask your director what he would recommend, or simply thank him for trying to help, and then look for someone else.

Above all, however, the most important thing to remember is that spiritual direction is a means for growth; it is not meant to involve handing over to your spiritual director the responsibility for your spiritual life. Keeping that in mind will, I believe, help you have realistic expectations and take intelligent advantage of everything God's providence offers you.

HOW CAN I STRENGTHEN MY WILL AND GROW IN HOLINESS?

We all need to remember that, when it comes to pursuing spiritual maturity, our own efforts are never enough. On the other hand, St. Thomas Aquinas reminded us many centuries ago that "grace builds on nature," and that means that we can do a lot to create a favorable climate for God's grace to be fruitful, to take root in our souls and bear abundant fruit, "some a hundredfold, some sixty, some thirty" (Matthew 13:8).

Forming the will—our capacity to make prudent, firm decisions and follow through with them in spite of opposition, temptation, or difficulty—is absolutely necessary for spiritual progress. A weak will inhibits our capacity to love, because love means self-giving, and self-giving is necessarily difficult in a fallen world, a world in which our fallen nature tends automatically toward self-indulgence.

Unfortunately, no flashy, romantic method exists for character formation. There are no shortcuts. I can, however, share some recommendations that spiritual writers have given throughout the centuries. It's up to each of us to put them into practice. But you will not be alone; three of the gifts of the Holy Spirit, which were planted in your soul at baptism, are directed toward giving your weak and wounded will a supernatural boost (these are the gifts of fortitude, piety, and fear of the Lord). So, if you make a decent effort to do your part, the Holy Spirit will surely give you a fantastic return for your investment. Your will has two jobs in the spiritual life. First, it has to submit to God, to embrace and obey God's will. Second, it has to govern your other, lower faculties (like your appetites) so they don't go off on their own and drag you into the muddy waters of laziness, lust, greed, and other vices. You can do some practical things to train your will in both tasks.

Job #1: Embracing God's Will

To embrace God's will for your life—whether in basic things like following the commandments and performing the duties of your state in life or in extraordinary moments when he sends special inspirations—you have to be convinced that God's will really is the very best option. This is the kind of conviction that drove St. Thomas More, for example, to give up the highest honors in the British kingdom, abundant riches, and an incomparable position of power and prestige, trading it all in for a few years in prison and a death sentence. He knew the answer to Christ's question: "What will it profit a man, if he gains the whole world and he forfeits his life?" (Matthew 16:26). The more deeply we are convinced that God's will, God's plan, and God's way are based on his infinite wisdom, limitless goodness, and passionate, personal love for us as individuals, the more we will want to embrace it and follow it, no matter the cost.

Deepening Your Conviction

How can you deepen that conviction? There is absolutely no better way to do so than by making mental prayer a part of your daily life. Add to mental prayer a good dose of daily spiritual reading, praying a rosary, and frequent reception of the sacraments of the Eucharist and confession, and you have a solid formula that will, gradually, deepen this conviction. It will become a solid foundation for a life of holiness and fruitfulness. But you must avoid just going through the motions in those spiritual disciplines; be faithful to them, and be faithful to constantly striving to do them better. The help of a good spiritual director is useful here. Go over each of your prayer commitments with your spiritual director. Explain what you do and how you do it, and ask for advice and tips on how to do it better.

Job #2: Self-Governance

The will's second job consists of governing your lower faculties. Your appetites always want to go toward their proper object, the particular pleasure associated with their exercise—food, sex, rest, entertainment. To strengthen your will, then, requires disciplining these appetites until, like a well-trained thoroughbred, they have learned to channel all their power in the direction that your will points them. This may take a long time. Our culture trains us in just the opposite way. Our consumerism actually debilitates the will in favor of the whims of emotion. Sometimes it takes prolonged periods of taxing effort to free the soul from the slavery of sentimentalism.

THE SECRET OF A SCHEDULE

The best tactic to employ for sure, albeit slow, progress in this area is by establishing and following a weekly and daily schedule that reflects your priorities and duties. If at any given hour of any given day you know what you are supposed to be doing, you give your willpower a huge advantage over your raucous appetites. When your appetites want to abandon your duty or commitment, you will recognize it immediately, because you can look at your schedule and see what your own, freely chosen life priority is right here and now.

For instance, if you are supposed to be working on your thesis and your appetites want to take a trip to a museum, you can look at your schedule and make an act of self-governance with your will, training your appetites by saying to yourself, "Well, okay, the Borromini exhibit is indeed worth seeing, but right now I can't just abandon the office; I have some deadlines to meet. But I have scheduled a time for some recreation on Saturday morning, so I can go to the exhibit then." That's self-governance; that's forming your will so that you are liberated from being a slave to your appetites.

Coming up with your weekly and daily schedule may not be easy for you, especially if you have a spontaneous temperament. But with the help of a friend (someone who likes to plan and organize things) or even with your spiritual director, you can do it. And then you will have to watch out for another pitfall: becoming a slave to your schedule! That will only cause you to be frustrated and tense all the time. Your schedule is a tool, a means to an end, but it can't foresee everything, so you have to maintain a certain flexibility. Balancing your freedom between the two types of slavery—to your whims or to your schedule—is the proper job of the virtue of prudence. And you will grow in this virtue only if you try, make mistakes, identify them, and keep on trying. For that, the daily examination of conscience can be invaluable.

Top Tips

Be sure to schedule your weekly day of rest, and honor that. Make sure to schedule free time to relax and enjoy the company of family and friends. We are not robots, after all. Schedule your times of prayer. Try and follow through on your commitments and decisions; exercising constancy is key for building willpower. If you want to make adjustments to your schedule or commitments, try to do so during your weekly review and planning session, not just on a whim.

Don't forget that forming your will is a long process. In fact, it's something you can never stop doing. Like a muscle, if you stop consciously exercising your willpower, it atrophies. Don't worry if you don't see much progress right away; don't worry if you keep falling back into slob-blob mode; just keep begging for God's help and plugging away, confident that you are glorifying God and building Christ's kingdom just by making a decent effort to serve him better. "But he who endures to the end will be saved" (Matthew 24:13).

Finally, remember that discouragement never comes from the Holy Spirit. Rather, it's a trick of the evil one. Scripture assures us, "With God all things are possible" (Matthew 19:26), and "[God's] mercy endures for ever" (Psalm 100:5).

Chapter Three

Overcoming Sin

SIN IS REBELLION AGAINST GOD. It is a denial of our status as God's creations and his children, dependent on him for our existence at every single moment. When we sin, we cut ourselves off from the very source of meaning, virtue, and happiness, both temporal and eternal. We become absurd and self-destructive, like trees uprooting themselves from the soil because they feel constrained by their roots. Sin disrupts, weakens, or ruptures our friendship with God. And since friendship with God is the whole purpose of our existence, sin is our archenemy, the source of all unhappiness and tragedy.

Today's culture tends to minimize and belittle sin. What matters to a hedonistic, relativistic consumer society is comfort and personal autonomy. Where does sin fit into an ethos like that? There is no eternal law to break, no universal moral order against which to rebel, no Father to offend. This poisonous ethos has a powerful ally inside each one of us: our fallen human nature. We have an enemy within. We tend toward self-centeredness (to which any parent of a two-year-old will eloquently attest).

But those of us who want to grow in our love for God know sin is real—and so is the battle to overcome it. In this chapter we'll look at the question of sin in light of the tools God has provided for us to overcome it.

HOW CAN I OVERCOME MY STRUGGLE WITH ANGER?
Anger is the most complex of all the human passions. It results when we experience an injustice, a pain, or an attack against our person of some

sort that we believe can be overcome. If we judge what we experience as something we cannot overcome, we simply feel deep sadness and painful resignation. But if we perceive that a bad thing is happening to us, and we think that our resistance to that bad thing can actually yield good results, we feel anger, and the feeling of anger moves us to act out against the perceived evil. If someone, for example, is insulting me and causing those around me to think badly of me, I may feel anger if I perceive that I can counteract the insults and turn the tables to save face. The feeling of anger will move me to retaliate, to defeat the insulting attack.

Anger is morally neutral—we just feel it because we are created that way; that's how human nature is designed. It becomes moral (righteous anger) or immoral (the sin of anger) depending on how we deal with the feeling. The feeling is meant to be governed by our reason (and as Christians, our reason is meant to be enlightened by our faith). If a coworker insults me unintentionally in a meeting, I will most likely feel anger welling up in my soul. If I choose to let that anger dictate my actions, I may lash out at my colleague, creating a scene, damaging a relationship, and disrupting whatever we were supposed to be working on. That's uncontrolled, unjustified, disproportionate anger—a form of self-centeredness. If I choose to rein in the feeling of anger through acts of patience and mercy, I avoid that damaging fallout, and I avoid the sin of anger.

If a person has habitually allowed free rein to their feelings of anger, instead of governing them with reason and faith, they will gradually form the vice of anger: a habitual disposition to commit the sin of anger. Some people have by nature a choleric and stormy temperament, and they have a kind of built-in tendency to fall into this sin and develop this vice. For those people, forming the virtues of patience and mercy (the virtues that govern the passion of anger) may be a lifelong struggle. But with God's grace, they *can* form those virtues. If the struggle is particularly hard, they will be crowned by our Lord with particular merit and give great glory to God through their spiritual battle.

WHY ARE SOME SINS SO HARD TO OVERCOME?

We have to remember that here on earth we are members of the Church militant. We are in the midst of a battle. As we grow spiritually, the enemies of our souls (the devil and his demons) don't sit idly by. Did you know that the Church's most notable heretics were almost all priests in their forties? Pelagius, Arius, Apollinaris, Nestorius—these were all men of God, passionately dedicated to the Church and seeking deeper intimacy with Christ, who advanced in theological knowledge and in the spiritual life. Who would have guessed that they would become instruments of ecclesial devastation and spiritual shipwreck? And yet, they did. We can never forget this: as we grow spiritually, the battle doesn't go away.

But the enemy of our souls is smart. He knows that temptation has to be customized to the situation of the person being tempted. The devil can't invent new sins (the seven capital sins are always the primary categories for sinful behavior), but he can disguise them in new ways. So, for someone who is well along the road toward spiritual maturity, the tempter instead seeks to clothe the capital sins in spiritual garments.

"Spiritualized" Capital Sins

For example, the inclination to vanity can appear in a subtle desire to have one's new and advanced piety noticed. You might start trying to draw attention to the outward manifestation of your devotion. Or you find yourself seeking to impress your spiritual director—hiding your real struggles, lest your director thinks you are less holy than you want to appear. You may even switch spiritual directors, not for any objective reason, but simply because you don't want to follow anyone's advice except your own.

The inclination to pride can show up in a sort of complacency in one's religious works. You think you are really doing well, and so you start planning all kinds of great spiritual projects, but you don't actually follow through on any of them. Or you start talking about spiritual things with other people just to give them advice, instead of seeking ways to put these lessons into practice yourself.

In the area of sensuality, one can become attached to the consolations that God has given during one's prayer and sacramental life. Maybe you find yourself trying to force certain emotional reactions during your meditation or after Communion. You start to seek spiritual feelings too much, forgetting that the goal of holiness is union with God in mind and will, not feelings of consolation. You can even begin to become attached to friendships or relationships that seem to be based on spiritual values, but in truth you invest in them because of the emotional payback you feel instead of the mutual spiritual support they are supposed to provide; this can become a kind of spiritual lust. Spiritual greed can take the form of an insatiable desire to read every spiritual book, to accumulate rosaries and holy cards and icons, to jump around from devotion to devotion trying to imbibe the entire spiritual patrimony of the Church all at once, even to the neglect of life's basic duties (like one's responsibilities to family members), instead of seeking patiently to go deep in the essentials.

"Thy Will Be Done—Not Mine!"

These types of attachments and self-absorption can hinder spiritual progress as much as the less subtle sins. But we need not become obsessed with them. As always in the spiritual life, the compass and anchor remain the same: I love God by accepting and fulfilling his will in each moment of my life. That's the litmus test, and that's the surest guide through the shadows and tangles of this earthly pilgrimage— as sure a guide for us as it was for Jesus: "My food is to do the will of him who sent me and to accomplish his work" (John 4:34).

WHAT IS A DISORDERED ATTACHMENT?

A disordered attachment is an emotional or psychological dependence on some person, object, or activity. It's a dependence on the object in question that's more than what reason would dictate. Reason, for human beings, gives us access to the proper measure of things—the measure in accordance with God's design.

Ordered Means "Reasonable"

For example, it is reasonable for adults to sleep seven hours a night on a regular basis. It's reasonable because that's more or less the amount of sleep that most people need in order to function in a healthy, normal way. If someone habitually sleeps twelve hours a night, something is probably wrong, and we would call this a disordered sleep pattern. It might stem from a physiological issue, but the cause might also be an emotional issue. In this case sleeping too much is an escape from reality in some way. And if that escape is a symptom of some unresolved violation of conscience that has made life unbearable, or simply a well-developed habit of laziness and indulgence, then it could very well be a disordered attachment: this person is overly dependent on sleep, using it as a shield to avoid facing the normal demands of life.

In any case, however, the standard for healthy dependence vs. unhealthy (disordered) dependence has to do with what is reasonable. What is reasonable is always related to—ordered to—the God-given purpose of the object in question. Sleep is meant to help us recover energy, not help us escape from responsibility.

As another example, it is reasonable to enjoy movies or sports as a form of recreation. We need relaxation and recreation to keep a healthy psychological and emotional balance. But when my football team's loss throws my life into disarray for an entire week, or when I can never miss watching a game, no matter what duties it may require me to neglect, I may have a disordered attachment to that form of recreation. If I spend twenty hours a week playing online video games and only three hours a week playing with my kids or enjoying time with my wife, it is safe to say that I am attached in an unreasonable, disordered way to video games.

Eating with Reason

Let's look at this issue as it relates to food. The purpose of food is nourishment. We are dependent on food for life, and life is a good thing, because we are created in God's image. The goodness of life is actually reflected in the pleasure that we get from eating good food. The pleasure is not evil or sinful; it is part of the nourishing experience; it is part of God's plan for life. We give glory to God by enjoying the good things of his creation! And so, it is reasonable to eat amounts and types of food necessary to stay properly nourished, and to enjoy eating them.

Of course, the actual amount will vary depending on the needs of individuals. A seven-foot lumberjack who fells trees nine hours a day will probably not have the same diet as a petite copyeditor.

We can know that we are deviating from the reasonable use of food if we habitually eat in such a way as to cause damage to our health. Overeating, or only indulging in the kinds of foods that give us the most pleasure, will interfere with the healthy functioning of our minds and bodies, instead of contributing to it. An unhealthy (disordered) attachment to food shows itself when eating is no longer ordered to enjoyable nourishment.

As in the case of sleep disorders, eating disorders can be symptoms of sinful self-indulgence (a manifestation of the root sin of sensuality), but they can also be symptoms of deeper problems. Habitual sins, for example, can lead to the disintegration of healthy self-respect and cause vanity or pride to show itself in making food or physical appearance into a kind of idol. On the other hand, emotional or psychological wounds, when unhealed by God's grace and his unconditional love, can fester in a person's soul and eventually manifest themselves in these types of disorders.

Attachments and Mortal Sins

Remember that for a sin to be mortal—in other words, for a sin to sever our friendship with Christ—three conditions are necessary. First, we have to be fully aware of the gravity of the sin. Second, we have to choose the sin with complete consent, not under any compulsion. Third, the matter of the sin has to be grave and serious in itself (stealing five dollars is not the same as stealing five million dollars).

In the case of overeating, for example, I would hesitate to say that the matter itself is grave, unless the amount is a direct and immediate threat to one's life. In related areas, however—the abuse of alcohol or drugs, for example—the matter *is* indeed grave. First of all, abusing those substances puts one's life (and others') in immediate danger, and secondly, when one purposely gets drunk or high, one knowingly forfeits or impairs the use of one's reason; one makes oneself less than human—in a sense, defacing the image of God.

Many struggle today with eating disorders. Almost always, these are compulsive behaviors. Other factors are subconsciously pushing someone to overeat, or undereat, or induce vomiting after eating. These root factors may be symptoms of sinful behavior that have wreaked havoc in a person's soul, in which case repentance will be needed to break the cycle. But they may also be the result of having suffered some sort of serious neglect or abuse, in which case the person is not culpable for the eating disorder, and healing will come through discovering the merciful and transforming love of God, which can repair any damage done by the sins of others.

HOW CAN I FORGIVE SOMEONE WHO SHOWS NO REMORSE?

Forgiveness is central to Christianity—so central that Jesus made it part of the prayer he taught us: "Forgive us our trespasses, as we forgive those who trespass against us." And this passage from Luke 17 is not the only passage in the New Testament on forgiveness. We need to read it in the context of the whole New Testament. When we do that, we see that Jesus never meant for us to hold a grudge until someone asks us for forgiveness.

Forgiving without Limits

The core of Our Lord's teaching in this area is that God's mercy is unconditional and unlimited, and so our mercy must be the same. This is clear from Jesus's parable of the unforgiving servant in Matthew 18. The king calls the servant in to pay a huge debt, but the servant can't pay it. So the king orders him and his family to be sold into slavery. The servant begs for clemency, and the king mercifully forgives the debt. Then that same servant runs across someone who owes him a much, much smaller debt, and treats him without any mercy at all. The king, infuriated, calls the servant back, reinstates his original debt, and sentences him to be tortured until he pays it back in full. Jesus then explains the moral of the story: "So also my heavenly Father will do to every one of you, if you do not forgive your brother from your heart" (Matthew 18:35).

When Jesus explains the Our Father, he makes the same point: "For if you forgive men their trespasses, your heavenly Father also will forgive you. But if you do not forgive men their trespasses, neither will your Father forgive your trespasses" (Matthew 6:14–15). Dying on the cross, Jesus didn't wait for his enemies to ask for forgiveness before forgiving them; while they crucified him he prayed for them: "Father, forgive them; for they know not what they do" (Luke 23:34). If he hadn't forgiven them himself, he could not have pleaded so mercifully on their behalf with the Father. And this unconditional forgiveness, which we receive from Jesus, is the model for how we are to forgive others: "Be kind to one another, tenderhearted, forgiving one another, as God in Christ forgave you" (Ephesians 4:32).

Forgiving and Being Forgiven

There is a difference between forgiving someone and that same someone receiving forgiveness. We can never force someone to receive our forgiveness, but we can still forgive that individual. If we forgive someone, he or she is forgiven—from our perspective. But if that person refuses to repent and take responsibility for the offense, it is impossible for he or she to receive that forgiveness. In that case, the person is not forgiven—from their perspective.

This helps us understand how God's mercy can be unlimited, yet some people don't experience it. It's not that God is holding it back; it's just that they are not open to receive it. I can offer you a glass of water, but if you don't take the glass, you won't quench your thirst. Forgiveness is like that. God doesn't wait for us to repent before he forgives us—his mercy is constant, overflowing, and limitless. But unless we repent, we will not receive that mercy, and we will remain unforgiven—just as someone who refuses to open their eyes remains in the dark.

The Danger of a Closed Heart

God is love. There is no one whom God does not love. There is no one to whom God does not offer his mercy. He holds no grudges. If we, then, consciously exclude someone from our love, from our mercy, by refusing to forgive, we are cutting ourselves off from God. We are telling God that we love him, but we don't love others whom he loves. So we are not in full communion with him. In that case, our hearts are closed toward certain people to whom God's heart is fully and constantly open. Here's how the *Catechism* explains it:

> Now—and this is daunting—this outpouring of mercy cannot penetrate our hearts as long as we have not forgiven those who have trespassed against us. Love, like the Body of Christ, is indivisible; we cannot love the God we cannot see if we do not love the brother or sister we do see. In refusing to forgive our brothers and sisters, our hearts are closed and their hardness makes them impervious to the Father's merciful love; but in confessing our sins, our hearts are opened to his grace. (*CCC* 2840)

The *Catechism* also stresses that this unconditional forgiveness is beyond our natural powers—we simply cannot live that depth of interior freedom without God's grace: "This crucial requirement of the covenant mystery is impossible for man. But 'with God all things are possible'" (*CCC* 2841). This is why forgiveness can be so hard. Our fallen nature tends toward self-righteousness, while our redeemed nature tends toward Christ-likeness. The battle between the two natures will rage as long as we are pilgrims on our way to the Father's house.

Forgiveness Goes Deeper Than Feelings

In this battle, it is critical to remember that true forgiveness does not always feel like forgiveness. I can truly forgive someone who has grossly offended me, but I may still experience strong emotions of anger, resentment, and just indignation. After all, if someone needs forgiveness, it's because they did something wrong, and someone was hurt because of it. Forgiving someone doesn't mean pretending that no damage was done or ignoring the destruction.

As we grow toward spiritual maturity, however, our emotional life will become more and more in sync with our spiritual life, and the best way to speed up this process is—in the arena of forgiveness—to pray for those who have offended us. To turn to the *Catechism* once again: "It is not in our power not to feel or to forget an offense; but the heart that offers itself to the Holy Spirit turns injury into compassion and purifies the memory in transforming the hurt into intercession" (*CCC* 2843).

WHAT SHOULD I DO IF I AM TEMPTED BY EVIL THOUGHTS?

When evil thoughts knock at the door of your mind, refuse to let them in. You may not be able to keep them from knocking, but by saying a short prayer ("Lord Jesus, have mercy on me.... Lord Jesus, I love you.... Sacred Heart of Jesus, I trust in you...") or praying a favorite line of Scripture ("Let it be done to me according to your word" [Luke 1:38], "Trust in him at all times" [Psalm 62:8], "The Lord is my light and my salvation, whom shall I fear?" [Psalm 27:1]), you may be able to resist letting them in. If they continue to clamor, continue to resist them: Make a visit to the Blessed Sacrament, go to confession, open your Bible and read the Word for fifteen minutes, do a work of mercy for someone, refocus on the task at hand.

Taking Captives

St. Paul explained that he took "every thought captive to obey Christ" (2 Corinthians 10:5). When God permits us to be barraged by evil thoughts, we can follow St. Paul's example. Even if we feel weak, we can still put up some resistance, which will eventually repel the spiritual attack: "Resist the devil, and he will flee from you" (James 4:7). And if our resistance takes the form of turning our thoughts to God—not just gritting our teeth and trying to exert massive self-control—then God will surely come to our rescue if we persevere: "Draw near to God, and he will draw near to you" (James 4:8). Sometimes the battle rages for long periods; God permits that in order to help us grow in virtue, self-knowledge, humility, and wisdom. Sometimes we must make strong, courageous decisions to resist the evil attacks, as St. Benedict did when he threw himself into a thorn bush in order to quench the fire of lustful temptations.

Being Responsible

On the other hand, if we are partially responsible for the origin of the evil thoughts, then we need to take the axe to the root and chop away. If we are filling our minds with worldly images and messages, or flirting with evil influences in what we listen to or how we spend our time, we are opening the door to evil thoughts. In a sense, we become their accomplices; we put ourselves in the path of sin. In this case, we can't expect God to remove the evil thoughts unless we repent and remove ourselves from the evil influences.

If we make a decent effort to resist, but the evil thoughts keep coming back and trying to invade our minds and hearts, we can trust that God knows what he is doing. He may be giving us a season of battle for our own sake, or for the sake of the Mystical Body of Christ, or both. We can continue to trust in him, and beg for the grace to persevere in our struggle to be faithful: "But he who endures to the end will be saved" (Matthew 24:13).

Less Ordinary Issues

In certain cases, these types of thoughts may also be related to an Obsessive-Compulsive Disorder (OCD). That type of disorder can also be exacerbated by spiritual attacks. If you are responsibly and determinedly utilizing the normal means to resist evil thoughts (like the means mentioned above) do not, over time, give you more strength and interior peace, there may a treatable disorder involved. But before going for a diagnosis, I would recommend meeting with a spiritual director to talk about the whole picture of your spiritual life.

Saints Struggle, Too

Even many of the saints struggled with blasphemous thoughts. St. Thérèse of Lisieux describes such attacks in her autobiography. St. Anthony Mary Claret had similar struggles. St. Ignatius of Loyola described how, in times of spiritual desolation, thoughts against Jesus or the Trinity assailed him. Detailed descriptions of these kinds of interior struggles are offered by the desert fathers, including St. Moses the Black and St. Anthony of the Desert.

The struggle against unwelcome evil thoughts can bring intense psychological and emotional pain. In such times of interior battle, the comfort of Christ-centered friendships can be a soothing balm and a secure refuge.

WHAT IS A "PROGRAM OF LIFE"?

One of the enemies of good spiritual direction is excessive subjectivity. We all have urgent personal issues that come and go; they occupy our attention and energy intensely for brief periods, but they really don't touch the deeper regions of our character and personality. When a child is sick, it preoccupies us. When someone at work is having problems that affect the rest of us, it preoccupies us. Sometimes issues like this are important enough to deserve ample attention during spiritual direction, but not usually. And yet, because they are on our mind, we will naturally tend to let them dominate our conversation during spiritual direction. This can inhibit us from the kind of deep, systematic, and structural work that spiritual direction is really designed to foster. The headlines of our lives change every day, just like the news headlines. But headlines are by nature superficial. We need to make sure that we don't waste all of our spiritual direction talking about superficial headlines. This is where the program of life comes in; it helps us to keep our ongoing spiritual work objective and profound.

To understand how it does that, we only have to understand what it is. The term "program of life" has some siblings: rule of life, reform of life, plan for spiritual growth, game plan for the soul, business plan for the soul, and so on. In all cases, the core meaning remains the same. The program of life is a tool that helps us personalize the principles of spiritual progress:

Prayer. Everyone needs to pray, but how often should I pray, what type of prayer should I focus on, what factors are making prayer hard for me? Every individual person, because of their life situation, background, education, and temperament will find individualized answers to those questions.

Virtue. Likewise, everyone needs to become more Christ-like through the practice of Christian virtue. But which virtues do I most need to develop and how exactly can I work on them, which habits of selfishness are most deeply rooted in me and how can I diminish them, what is the underlying cause of my most frequent sins and faults? Again, every individual will answer these questions differently.

State in Life. The same goes for the fulfillment of God's will through fidelity to the responsibilities of one's state in life. Every father needs to guide, discipline, and spend time with his children; every husband needs to give his life for his wife, as Christ gave his life for the Church; every professional needs to be another Christ in their workplace—but these ideals will take on unique (and uniquely beautiful) characteristics as they are incarnated in the unique and dynamic reality of every individual.

The program of life consists of the personalized answers to all these questions, phrased and arranged in such a way that they become a guide for daily living.

Your Spiritual Workout Program

The program of life, then, is like a spiritual workout program that insures spiritual growth because it is customized to the individual's needs and opportunities. When we meet with our spiritual director, it is good to start by going over the headlines, but reviewing together the main points of the program of life is the real path to consistent, substantial progress.

Three other things are worth noting.

1. When we draw up a program of life together with our spiritual director (which is a very good idea), our efforts to follow it have the added benefit of being acts of obedience, since we are doing not just our own will, but God's will as manifested through our director (we are not speaking of a vow of obedience, but the virtue). An effective time to draw up a program of life is during a retreat; a little distance from the daily grind sharpens our spiritual vision.

2. A good program of life includes a personal (usually weekly) schedule with prayer commitments that are decided upon ahead of time. This saves us from the inconsistency that comes from moodiness and constant improvisation. It also includes concrete areas of activity (the formation of good habits of behavior) that directly counteract the most salient manifestations of one's root sin.

3. The program of life is a living entity. It can and should change as we get to know ourselves better and as we grow. Living it out is not like following the Ten Commandments, to which there are never exceptions. Rather, it's like following a game plan on the basketball court; flexibility in the face of life's dynamism is preferable to scrupulosity.

HOW CAN I IDENTIFY MY ROOT SIN?

This is a great question, because a program of life is ineffective without having identified your root sin. Unless you understand the dynamism underlying your frequent faults and failings, you will never be able to work intelligently to overcome them. It's like gardening. If you want to get rid of the weeds, you can't just pull out the stems; you have to get at the roots. Otherwise, progress is short-lived and unsubstantial, and sooner or later discouragement and frustration set in.

In trying to identify your root sin, the wisdom of the Church comes in handy. Spiritual writers through the ages have identified three possible candidates. Before I describe them, however, it behooves us to make one clarification. All of us, simply because of our fallen human nature, have sinful tendencies linked to all three of the candidates. Saying that we have a root sin simply means that for each of us, one of the three is dominant. It's bigger than the others and exerts greater influence on our day-to-day behavior.

That said, here are the three possible root sins: pride, vanity, and sensuality. Pride, in this sense, refers to a disordered attachment to our own excellence. The proud person tends to seek meaning and fulfillment in his or her own achievements and conquests. Vanity is a disordered attachment to the approval of other people. The vain person tends to seek meaning and fulfillment in being appreciated or liked by others. Sensuality is a disordered attachment to comfort, ease, and pleasure. The sensual person tends to seek meaning and fulfillment in taking it easy and simply enjoying life.

Notice that each of these root sins is a disordered attachment to something. The things in themselves—achievements, relationships, pleasures—are not evil. The problem comes when we seek meaning and fulfillment in those temporal, created realities. In fact, we are created and called to seek our meaning and fulfillment in God alone, in our ever-deepening relationship with him. Achievements, relationships, and pleasures are meant to be ordered around and toward that principle and foundation of our life. As the *Catechism* puts it:

> The desire for God is written in the human heart, because man is created by God and for God; and God never ceases to draw man to himself. Only in God will he find the truth and happiness he never stops searching for. (*CCC* 27)

Again, it is important to realize that we each have tendencies that spring from pride, vanity, and sensuality. None of us is exempt from any of them, because we all have inherited a fallen human nature. But in each of us, one of the three is usually dominant. If we can identify which one, we can better aim our efforts to grow spiritually; we can strive to develop the virtues that counteract the cause, the root, of our falls and faults. We can identify this root sin, also called "dominant defect" by some spiritual writers, by looking at the common manifestations of each. The manifestations which are strongest in your life can clue you in to your root sin.

Below you will find a list of these common manifestations. Read through them once quickly and make a note of the ones that characterize you most. You will find that sometimes you fall into all of them, but some of them will jump out at you as particularly common or strong in your life. Whichever of the three has more of those is most likely your root sin. As you go through this exercise, you may find it more difficult than you anticipated. That's because self-knowledge is slippery. (That's one of the most compelling reasons for finding a spiritual director to help us be objective in our spiritual work.)

Common Manifestations of Pride

- too high an opinion of myself
- annoyance with those who contradict me
- anger if I don't get my way or am not taken into account
- easily judgmental, putting others down, gossiping about them
- slow to recognize my own mistakes or notice when I hurt others
- inability to seek and give forgiveness
- rage when others don't thank me for favors
- unwillingness to serve, rebellion against what I don't like
- impatience, distance, brusqueness in my daily contact with others
- thinking I am the only one who knows how to do things right, unwillingness to let others help
- inflated idea of my own intelligence and understanding, dismissing what I do not understand or what others see differently
- not feeling a need for God, even though I might pray
- nursing grudges, even in small matters
- resistance to taking orders from authority
- inflexible in preferences
- always putting myself and my things first, indifference toward others and their needs, never putting myself out for them
- centering everything (conversation, choices) on myself and my likes
- calculating in my relationship with God and with others

Common Manifestations of Vanity

- always seeking admiration and praise, worrying about not getting it
- excessive concern about physical appearance
- being guided by the opinions of others rather than principle
- some types of shyness
- sacrificing principles in order to fit in
- placing too much a premium on popularity and acceptance
- easily discouraged at my failures
- taking pleasure in listening to gossip and hearing about others' failures

- always wanting to be the center of attention, at times stretching the truth, or lying outright, or being uncharitable in my words in order to achieve this

Common Manifestations of Sensuality
- laziness
- always doing the most comfortable, what requires least effort
- not going the extra mile for others
- procrastination, last-minute in everything
- shoddiness, complaining, excessively affected by minor discomforts
- inability to sacrifice
- not doing my part at home
- expecting everyone else to serve me
- behavior and decisions ruled by my feelings and moods instead of my principles
- frequent daydreaming with self at the center
- unable to control my thoughts when they attract me, even if they are not good
- doing only what I enjoy (choice of food, work, and so on)
- uncontrolled and overpowering curiosity, wanting to see and experience everything and every pleasure
- allowing my senses and impulses overrule what I know is right and wrong
- acting out my feelings (frustrations, desires) with no regard for my conscience, God, or others
- only working with those I like, being easily hurt
- fickleness and inconstancy
- inability to finish what I start

WHAT IS THE DIFFERENCE BETWEEN CAPITAL SIN AND ROOT SIN?

This question illustrates how rich our Catholic faith really is. It transcends our ability to comprehend it; there is always more for us to discover. This is why the concept of root sins can be approached, explained, and understood from different perspectives, just as a diamond shows forth its beauty through many different facets. The different facets don't contradict each other; they actually enrich the diamond's beauty. The apparent contradiction between a seven-way and a three-way categorization of the root sins can be understood like that.

Welcoming the Spiritual Wealth

But before I explain how, I want to illustrate this point with a different topic. The *Catechism* circles back to key ideas frequently. For example, in 45, it teaches us the purpose of human existence: "Man is made to live in communion with God in whom he finds happiness." That simple sentence is like an atomic bomb: small, yet immensely powerful. But later, in 1721, the *Catechism* gives an apparently different explanation of the purpose of human existence: "God put us in the world to know, to love, and to serve him, and so to come to paradise."

Is there really a contradiction here? In the words, yes; in the *meaning* of the words, no. The reality of our purpose as human beings is something so wonderful, deep, and multifaceted that it can be described in myriad ways, as can many other aspects of God's revelation. Whenever we begin to use our intelligence to delve into the deeper meaning of our faith, we must keep this in mind. Otherwise, we may become unduly attached to certain formulations, thereby missing the point. Throughout the Church's history, such undue attachments have yielded extremely bitter fruit—heresies, schisms, libels, executions, and riots, to name a few.

Deriving Seven from Three

Now, back to root sins. The section of the *Catechism* that deals with the seven capital sins is discussing the concept of vice. Vices are the opposite of virtues. Where virtues are habitual behavior patterns in harmony with God's will and purpose for our lives, vices are habitual behavior patterns contradicting that purpose. The *Catechism* explains that "the repetition of sins...engenders vices, among which are the capital sins" (1876). Categorizing vices according to the capital sins goes way back in our Catholic tradition, and even reflects philosophical ethics as taught by Plato and Aristotle. These vices are called "capital" because they give rise to so many other sins (*caput* in Latin means "head" or "source"). If I allow myself to be carried away by anger, for example, I may commit vengeance through murder. If I covet someone's position at work, I may slander them so that their boss fires them. The murder or the slander are sinful results of other, capital sins.

When speaking of root sins, however, spiritual writers are looking at the deep-seated tendencies toward selfishness that we have inherited because of original sin. These are tendencies to seek our happiness outside of communion with God. They are not vices per se, because they didn't come about as the result of repeated personal sins. Rather, they make up the raw material from which vices spring. We can correct vices by forming virtues, but we can never completely eradicate (de-root) our tendencies to selfishness. They always remain to be battled against.

The capital vices, in fact, flow from those self-centered tendencies, those root sins. Gluttony (inordinate attachment to the pleasures of food and drink), slothfulness (inordinate attachment to comfort and ease), and lust (inordinate attachment to sexual pleasure) grow out of the root sin of sensuality. Each of them seeks happiness through material goods or experiences. Envy (willful resentment of another's success or good fortune) and covetousness (willful desire to possess what rightfully belongs to others) can flow from vanity (seeking fulfillment from the approval and praise of other people) if the reason I resent others, for example, is because they get more attention than I do. But they can also flow from pride (seeking fulfillment in my own excellence and achievements) if my reason for desiring another person's position, for example, is because I want to assert my superiority over that person. Just to make things more complicated, covetousness can also be a manifestation of sensuality: I can be greedy because I simply want to enjoy life instead of having to work hard all the time. This slippery nature of covetousness is one reason St. Paul reminds us that "the love of money is the root of all evils" (1 Timothy 6:10).

By now, if you aren't thoroughly confused (and here we have just been scratching the theological surface: St. Thomas Aquinas's *Summa Theologiae* catalogues more than a hundred vices and virtues, and also, by the way, ends up tracing *every* vice and sin back to pride), you will probably have perceived why many spiritual writers encourage us to focus on the three root sins. If we just focus on counteracting the vices themselves, we may simply be snapping off branches from the stubborn weed of selfishness, instead of whittling down its trunk.

In the end, however, the main reason for trying to categorize the different types of sins (vices) and the disordered tendencies which gives rise to them (root sins) is to help us work intelligently in our efforts to follow Christ more closely. To that end, you should feel free to use whichever categorization helps you most.

WHY IS IT IMPORTANT TO GO TO CONFESSION FREQUENTLY?

There is a widespread bad habit that thinks confession only exists for those times when we sin so grievously that we experience a spiritual earthquake. Without a doubt, this is the primary purpose of the sacrament—to open a way of reconciliation for a baptized Christian who has fallen into grave sin. But popes and spiritual writers in recent centuries have repeatedly and energetically encouraged all of us to practice frequent, regular confession. Blessed Mother Teresa of Calcutta used to go to confession weekly, as did Pope John Paul II. Obviously, these giants of the faith weren't confessing mortal sins every week, so what was the reasoning behind their practice of frequent, regular confession?

Benefits of Frequent Confession

Every sacrament imparts its own particular grace. The sacramental grace of confession is primarily the forgiveness of sins, but it is also, secondarily, the spiritual strengthening of the soul. This is why it is called a sacrament of healing. It heals (reconciles) our relationships with God and with the Church, which have been wounded or broken by personal sin, and at the same time it strengthens those relationships. When we break a bone, the body will repair it with an extra dose of calcium, so that the bone is actually stronger at the break point after the healing than it was before the injury. Something similar happens with confession. God pours out his strengthening grace in a special way on the aspects of our spiritual organism, so to speak, that we present to him in confession.

This is why the devil works so hard to keep us away from frequent, regular confession. If our relationship with God has been ruptured (by mortal sin), he doesn't want it reconciled. But even if it has just been wounded (venial sin), he doesn't want it strengthened.

This sacrament, however, proffers even more benefits to the soul than the sacramental graces of forgiveness and strengthening. Making a good confession requires the arduous task of self-reflection. All spiritual writers agree that ongoing self-examination is a basic ingredient in spiritual progress. We have to discover, with God's help, how miserable and needy we really are, spiritually speaking, in order to open ourselves confidently and eagerly to God's action.

Going to confession is also like doing a major spiritual workout. Through the process of self-examination, repentance, confession, and penance, we exercise every major spiritual muscle group: the theological virtues (faith, hope, love for God), humility (it's not exactly self-inflating to kneel down and systematically expose our faults and failings), justice, prudence, fortitude (it takes courage to step into a confessional), and self-denial. This sacrament is like a gymnasium of Christian virtue. Frequent and regular workouts therein will do wonders for our spiritual health.

What to Confess?

Any valid confession will inundate your soul with these benefits, and the more conscientiously you participate in the sacrament, the better your workout will be. To be valid, a confession needs both sincere repentance (which includes the intention of fulfilling your assigned penance) and the actual confession of sin. When we have obvious sins on our conscience, that it is easy. But as we grow in the spiritual life, the obvious sins tend to diminish. When that happens, we need to examine ourselves more carefully to uncover the hidden attitudes, judgments, and intentions that are still self-centered and not Christ-centered. Scripture warns us that we do not know how deep our selfishness goes: "But who can discern his errors? / Clear me from hidden faults" (Psalm 19:12). This is an excellent topic to discuss in spiritual direction.

Yet sometimes we identify failings that were not willful; we just fell into them out of weakness or lack of reflection. Here we can enter a gray area between venial sin, for which we are in some way directly responsible, and what spiritual writers call "imperfections," for which we are only remotely responsible, if at all. A good example of this is internally judging and criticizing other people. Sometimes we notice ourselves doing that only after we have already been doing it for a few minutes; we didn't really consciously decide to start judging them. It is an injustice, but it stems from deep-seated selfish tendencies, not a willful lack of charity (unless we keep doing it even after we notice we were doing it).

When the material of confession is in this gray area, it is a healthy practice to end the confession by referring to some past sins that were more obvious. If they have already been confessed, we don't need to confess them again in detail (that would be a step toward scrupulosity), but bringing them anew to the Lord is an excellent way to show him that we are truly sorry for all of our sins and failings. So, for example, if in the past your obvious sins had to do with theft, bribery, or fraud, you could finish your regular confession now by saying something like, "I confess these sins [the ones you have already mentioned] and all the sins of my past life, especially those against the virtue of justice. These are my sins."

Now that we have explored some theoretical and practical aspects of regular, frequent confession, you may be wondering, "How frequent and regular should my confession be?" If Mother Teresa and John Paul II went weekly, that's not a bad yardstick. But that's not always practical, and it may make you feel pressured. Confession every two weeks will be a turbo boost to your friendship with Christ, and, in today's corrosive culture, monthly confession is almost the minimum required for someone who is serious about spiritual progress. But remember, the Church only requires us to go to confession annually, or if we have a mortal sin on our conscience. Frequent confession is not a duty imposed by the Church; it is simply a heartfelt, wise recommendation.

WHAT IS THE EXAMINATION OF CONSCIENCE (AND WHY IS IT IMPORTANT)?

The examination of conscience is a critical issue for deepening one's friendship with Christ. Hands down, this spiritual discipline is a central plank in the platform leading to progress in spiritual maturity for both religious and laity.

You are probably more familiar with this concept than you think. Every time you go to confession, you prepare for the sacrament by examining your conscience. That's how you identify your sins and failings, so you can confess them. So don't think you are starting from scratch when it comes to making this practice part of your daily spiritual program.

The Why

The daily examination of conscience helps remove something that all spiritual writers agree is one of the most common obstacles to substantial growth in holiness (which includes basic human maturity): the lack of self-knowledge. This is so obvious that it is often overlooked. If you want to get to San Francisco, you can't plot an intelligent route unless you know where you are starting from, where you are right now. If you want to win an Olympic gold medal, you have to build on your strengths, which come naturally, but you also have to correct, shore up, and improve on your weak points. And you can't do that if you don't know what those are, or if you refuse to look at them squarely and honestly.

When it comes to deepening our relationship with God, those natural and obvious reasons for knowing ourselves thoroughly and sincerely are bolstered with a supernatural reason. The life of a Christian is built upon the foundation of grace, of God's action in our lives. We will only build on that foundation if we truly understand how little we can do to overcome our selfish tendencies and grow in Christlike love (the heart of holiness and happiness). And we can understand and accept the immensity of our need for God's grace and mercy only insofar as we come to grips with the immensity of our weakness and misery, which requires authentic, systematic self-knowledge.

The How

The daily examination of conscience is like a mini-meditation. At first, set aside five minutes (later you may want to increase this to ten) toward the end of the day. Religious do it during compline, the last hour of the divine office (the liturgy of the hours), usually prayed right before going to bed. But St. Francis de Sales recommended that busy laypeople try to squeeze it in before the evening meal, simply because tiredness can be such an impediment later at night. If you happen to be the person who prepares the evening meal, you may want to make a deal with the rest of the family so they do the dishes while you sneak off for five minutes and do your conscience examen.

What happens during these five minutes can vary in particulars, but the essence is always the same: prayer reflection on how God has acted in your life throughout the day and how you have responded. There are three parts to this prayer reflection: a beginning, a middle, and an end.

The Beginning. To begin, make the sign of the cross and remind yourself that you are in the presence of God, your Father, who loves you with a personal, determined, and everlasting love. Ask the Holy Spirit to enlighten you, so you can know yourself better in order to give yourself more fully to God. You can do this in your own words, or you can use a prayer like this one:

O Holy Spirit, come in Thy mercy;
enlighten my mind and strengthen my will
that I may know my sins,
humbly confess them,
and sincerely amend my life.

The Middle. The middle of the examination of conscience consists in serenely and prayerfully looking over your day. It's like taking a helicopter flight back over ground you've covered on foot. You want to keep an eye out for two things especially: moments of victory and moments of failure.

Victories are moments when God's grace triumphed in your behavior (you didn't lose your patience in a situation where you usually do), or when his grace embraced and enfolded you in a special way (he gave you an intimate awareness of his goodness while you did your morning meditation). When you find these victories, smile at them, enjoy them, and thank God for them.

Failures are the opposite: moments when you cut yourself off from God's grace, willfully or simply through weakness and distraction; moments when you did not image God's goodness in your thoughts, words, and behavior; moments when you sinned by commission or omission. As you spot these failures, you should allow yourself to mourn them ("Blessed are those who mourn, for they shall be comforted," as it says in Matthew 5:4), but never give in to discouragement. Instead, always turn discouragement into humility. Don't think: "I am such a selfish wreck; I am not making any progress." Instead, pray: "You see, Lord, how weak I am, and how much I need your grace!"

As you look for victories and failures, it helps to keep a special eye out for the points that are included in your program of life (a specific plan for building virtues and overcoming root sins). In this way, you will become more familiar with the manifestations of your root sin, and this will enable you (gradually) to respond more quickly and virtuously to difficult situations and temptations.

At the same time, however, allow yourself to dig beneath the surface. When you spot a victory or a failure, ask yourself, *Why did I lose my patience again, when I really didn't want to?* or *Why did my meditation this morning go so much better than usual?* As you reflect on the causes of your behavior, with the guidance of the Holy Spirit, your self-knowledge increases significantly.

The End. You always want to conclude the examination of conscience with two things:

1. A renewal of your commitment to try and follow Christ faithfully tomorrow. This can be a general renewal, or you can formulate some kind of a specific resolution—for example, you might say, "Lord, tomorrow, with your help, I don't want to gossip during our lunch party, so please help me to change the subject when it starts, or at least give me the strength to walk away."

2. An act of contrition telling God you are sorry for your sins. This doesn't have to be a formal act of contrition (you can use your own words), but sometimes it helps to use a simple formula. For example, you can use the act of contrition utilized at the end of confession, or the "I confess to almighty God…" prayer we utilize at the beginning of Mass.

This may seem like an incredibly complicated way to spend five minutes, but in reality it isn't. You will find your own rhythm, and the Holy

Spirit will help you. The important thing is to make this examination of conscience a staple of your daily diet. If you find it hard at first because your mind is racing, you may want to try doing it in writing. First, write down two specific things you are thankful for from the day, and then write down one thing about your behavior from the day that you would change if you could go back in time. Finally, write down a petition for the grace to follow Christ faithfully tomorrow.

Chapter Four

Life in the World

WE ARE MEANT TO LIVE joyfully here on earth, fully human and fully alive. That's not always easy for us today, but in this chapter we'll examine how our Catholic faith can help us deal with life's practicalities as well as live the Church's liturgical seasons more richly. The questions and answers in this section cover a variety of topics, but the end result is the same: a vibrant life of holiness and wholeness enabling us to shine as bright lights to those around us.

WHAT KIND OF ENTERTAINMENT IS APPROPRIATE?

Art and entertainment are meant to serve a noble, useful, and lovely purpose for us human beings. History is eloquent on this point. Ever since there have been human communities, there has been entertainment. Epic stories, transmitted orally long before they were written down, were already in existence at the very dawn of civilization. The dramatic arts, the performance arts, and the plastic arts emerged in conjunction with religious rituals and beliefs. Athletic contests, another form of entertainment, were already highly developed by the time the city of Rome was founded in 753 B.C. The delight we experience through enjoying works of art and entertainment touches something near to the core of human nature.

What is the purpose of that delight? Why did God give us sensitivity, a capacity to enjoy these pastimes? This is the most important question. If we can identify the purpose of entertainment, from God's perspective, we can then determine which products, which kinds of entertainment, we should choose to enjoy.

The Power and Purpose of Entertainment

Art and entertainment move the heart. They give us an experience of beauty and truth that touches every part of our human soul: our intelligence (they engage our mind), our emotional world (they stimulate powerful feelings), and our will (they stir up or reinforce certain desires). Take the story of Cinderella, for example. As we read or watch or listen to that story, our minds resound with the truth of justice as the evil stepsisters tried to imprison Cinderella, but the prince set her free; our emotions vibrate with sadness at Cinderella's plight, with hope when the fairy godmother appears, with fear when the clock strikes midnight, with utter joy when the prince sets out with courage and determination to find the foot that fits the glass slipper; and our wills then desire to promote justice, to continue hoping, to be courageous and determined. At the end of the story, we have been instructed, reminded, nourished—the values embodied in the story are strengthened in our hearts. This is the power of art and entertainment!

A work of art or entertainment that is pleasing and attractive, then, is kind of like a Trojan horse: It causes those values contained within it to enter into and echo within our own hearts. When we swallow the pleasure, we also swallow, at least a little bit, the worldview.

As a result, if we allow ourselves to be repeatedly entertained by songs, stories, and images that are pleasing to consume but contain anti-values, or anti-Christian values, on the inside, we put our souls in danger. Junk food is okay every once in a while, because it tastes good. But if we make ice cream and potato chips into the staples of our diet, our health is going to suffer; those foods are pleasing to eat, but they contain more transfats than they contain vitamins.

St. Paul presents this principle clearly and beautifully in Philippians 4:8: "Finally, brethren, whatever is true, whatever is honorable, whatever is just, whatever is pure, whatever is lovely, whatever is gracious, if there is anything worthy of praise, think about these things."

Avoiding Immorality and Being Realistic

Also important are two other related observations. First, certain types of entertainment are intrinsically evil—that is, the actual substance of the entertainment, the stuff that causes the pleasure, is immoral. As followers of Christ, we can never use or support or even tolerate these kinds of entertainment. This was the case with the ancient gladiator fights. The thrill that the spectators experienced came from the mortal danger the contestants faced: The combatants fought to the death. But human life is too precious for that! To make killing into a spectator sport directly contradicts human dignity. When the Roman Empire became Christian, this form of entertainment eventually was abolished.

In our day, the most obvious example of immoral entertainment is pornography and all its related industries (such as strip clubs, prostitution, human trafficking, sex tourism). This is a subset of the entertainment industry that treats human beings like products, like consumer goods to be bought, used, and thrown away.

Second, many works of art or entertainment are not explicitly Christian or Catholic, yet they present, in some form or other, authentic values. In the first centuries of the Christian era, theologians and philosophers argued extensively about whether Christians should read and study the classical works of literature and philosophy. The works of Cicero, Plato, Thucydides, Virgil—these were pagan works, written by pagans for pagans. They did not present Christ; they did not present a Christian worldview. Because of this, many theologians believed that Christians should not read them. In the end, however, the Church realized that these towering achievements of the human spirit, even though they were not explicitly Christian, contained much that was "true, honorable, just, pure, lovely, gracious, excellent, and worthy of praise." And so, not only did we keep reading them, Catholic monks were actually the ones who helped preserve them from obliteration during the Dark Ages.

Today our society is, in many ways, a neopagan society. As a result, much of our art and entertainment no longer presents an explicitly Christian worldview. Yet, as in the case of the ancient classics, it may contain much that can inspire and edify us, even while it entertain us.

A Word about TV Shows that Involve Contact with the Spirit World

Certain shows present the world of ghosts and spirits as a kind of extension of this material world. This materialistic view of the spirit world is reminiscent of the ancient pagan afterlife. As a result, repeatedly watching shows like this could easily, although subtly, make a Christian start thinking of the afterlife in pagan terms. That would be dangerous, because the pagan view of the afterlife obscures the reality of spiritual warfare that Christianity makes so clear to us.

If the show itself doesn't promote real occult practices, which would definitely make it objectionable, and if the human drama is depicted in a way which promotes authentic virtues (courage, wisdom, prudence, justice, fidelity, purity)—in other words, if the protagonists succeed because of those virtues—I can see how someone would consider watching such a show no less offensive than reading ancient Greek dramas like *Medea* or *Antigone* (not that I am suggesting such shows would be of the same literary quality as those plays!).

Drawing the Line

The real question is something like this: *When I am honest with myself, do I see my view of the afterlife being paganized a little bit by watching this particular show?* If the answer to that question is yes, then it would be best to find another favorite show. Your reflection might continue:

> *I have a few hours each week that I can spend enjoying some entertainment. I know that the purpose of entertainment is to help me relax, and at the same time to inspire and edify me—if I get some relaxation, inspiration, and edification every week, I am better able to keep "fighting the good fight" of my faith (see 1 Timothy*

6:12). So, does this show provide me with enough relaxation, inspiration, and edification to be worthy of me spending an hour of my time watching it? Would something else be a better investment?

WHAT DOES THE CHURCH SAY ABOUT END-OF-LIFE ISSUES?

The Church offers solid principles regarding end-of-life issues, but it is not always easy to apply those principles to particular situations. Let me review the principles, then reflect a little bit on how they might apply to someone's final days or weeks on earth, when he or she can no longer eat or drink.

Guiding Principles

Because each of us is created in God's image and invited to everlasting friendship with God, human life is sacred. Because of this human dignity, it is never justified to directly will or cause the death of an innocent person, nor is it justified to purposely try to damage or lessen the quality of a person's life (through maiming or kidnapping, for example). To defend this sacred dignity of human life, the Church has always taught that abortion and euthanasia (direct killing in order to alleviate suffering) are morally wrong, just as wrong as any other form of murder.

Nevertheless, in this fallen world, death is inevitable. At some point, we all will die. When it becomes clear that someone is dying, therefore, we do not have a moral obligation to do everything possible to extend their life as long as possible. Now, in some cases, there may be a particular reason why we would indeed want to keep someone alive, even at great cost or pain. For example, take the case of a father and son who have been estranged for decades and live on different sides of the globe. The father is facing heart failure, and the doctors agree that intervention at this point would most likely be useless, though some extreme measures may keep the heart functioning for another couple of weeks or a month. The family members, or the father himself, may request that those extreme measures be taken, so that the estranged son can have time to travel to the hospital, in hopes of a final reconciliation. That particular family may decide to use aggressive treatments, whereas a family already at peace may not. Each would be justified.

Accepting the inevitable, however, does not mean abandoning a dying person or hastening their death. That would constitute willing that a person die, just to get it over with, rather than humbly accepting death as a natural end of life. Therefore, if someone is dying, it would be immoral to willingly deny them the fundamental necessities that we owe to every human being: shelter, clothing, basic nutrition, and hydration. In many cases, as a person is dying, their system will no longer accept nutrition and hydration. If that's the case, it would most often be futile and disproportionate to try and force-feed them. In some cases, the dying process is so painful that the amount or type of palliative medicine required to relieve the pain may actually hasten the death. Nevertheless, such palliative care is acceptable (indeed, even an expression of love), if the person truly is dying. Again, however, if the dying person wants to remain alert in order to be able to converse with an estranged family member, for example, they may choose to forego pain relievers.

Those are the basic principles: the sacredness of human life, the inevitability of death, the moral duty to provide basic necessities, when possible, but not to provide futile or disproportionate treatments. Here is how the *Catechism of the Catholic Church* summarizes the issue:

> Discontinuing medical procedures that are burdensome, dangerous, extraordinary, or disproportionate to the expected outcome can be legitimate; it is the refusal of "over-zealous" treatment. Here one does not will to cause death; one's inability to impede it is merely accepted. The decisions should be made by the patient if he is competent and able or, if not, by those legally entitled to act for the patient, whose reasonable will and legitimate interests must always be respected.

Even if death is thought imminent, the ordinary care owed to a sick person cannot be legitimately interrupted. The use of painkillers to alleviate the sufferings of the dying, even at the risk of shortening their days, can be morally in conformity with human dignity if death is not willed as either an end or a means, but only foreseen and tolerated as inevitable. Palliative care is a special form of disinterested charity. As such it should be encouraged. (*CCC* 2278–2279)

Practical Conclusions

As you can see, moral decisions are not always clear, and they are not always easy. This is one reason it is so important for the mature Catholic to make a strong commitment to ongoing formation. What we learned in CCD and what we hear on Sundays often is simply insufficient for the battles of life in the modern world. Our Church has a vast treasure of wisdom and the most dependable moral guidance available on earth, but it doesn't translate well into sound bites. We need to keep ourselves informed. We need to be as responsible and proactive in this area as we are with our professional life or with our favorite hobbies. As a priest, I can honestly say that it can be nothing less than heart-wrenching to see adult Catholics—intelligent, well-adjustment human beings—facing life's major crises with only a rudimentary knowledge of their faith.

HOW CAN I BETTER PREPARE FOR LENT?

You have no idea what God has in store for you this Lent (but God does, and he is looking forward to it!). On the other hand, you do know that God has chosen to work in our souls through the Liturgy, and that includes the liturgical seasons. So preparing for Lent means getting ready to hear and heed what God wants to say to you during those days. The Church gives us three general directives in this regard.

Intensify your prayer life. Start thinking now about how you can do this. It's a good topic to talk about in spiritual direction. Do you need to increase your Eucharistic life, give more discipline to your personal prayer time, inculcate family prayer time, go on a retreat? God will put something on your heart. But be realistic. Don't let your eyes be bigger than your stomach (in the spiritual sense).

Embrace the cross. Lent is a penitential season, a time when we remember how self-centered we have been and tend to be, and renew our commitment and efforts at repenting and growing in Christian love. This is the origin of the tradition of giving something up for Lent. The idea is to make a sacrifice, denying our naturally self-indulgent tendencies in some way in order to unite ourselves more fully to Christ's redeeming sacrifice on Calvary. This is not merely a self-help kind of resolution. It is a self-offering to God: "Lord, many times I have chosen to do my own will instead of yours. By offering this sacrifice I want to learn to take up my cross, to say yes to you and your will, following in Jesus's footsteps." Whatever we give up (watching sports, eating dessert) or take on (daily Mass, weekly Way of the Cross) as our Lenten sacrifice (again, be realistic), the key is to give it that truly Christ-centered meaning.

Practice Christian charity. Lent is a time to prepare for the fruitful celebration of the Lord's passion, death, and resurrection during Holy Week. That Paschal Mystery was God's unfathomable and amazing testimony of love for us sinners. There is no better way to get in tune with that self-forgetful and self-sacrificial love than by imitating it. During Lent we should make a special point of serving our neighbors—but here again, be realistic. Here the traditional corporal works of mercy can spark ideas. The *Catechism* reminds us of them:

> Instructing, advising, consoling, comforting are spiritual works of mercy, as are forgiving and bearing wrongs patiently. The corporal works of mercy consist especially in feeding the hungry, sheltering the homeless, clothing the naked, visiting the sick and imprisoned, and burying the dead. Among all these, giving alms

to the poor is one of the chief witnesses to fraternal charity: it is also a work of justice pleasing to God. (*CCC* 2447)

Something in the air of spring brings out new buds, new branches, new life. The word *Lent* has its etymological roots in an Old English word meaning "spring." Something in the air of Lent will bring out new buds, new branches, new life in our relationship with Christ—we just have to open up some windows.

HOW CAN I CELEBRATE THE SEASON OF EASTER MORE FULLY?

Ever since I was ordained, I have been struck every year by the decrease in daily Mass attendance as soon as Lent ends. I am not trying to say that everyone is obliged to go to Mass on a daily basis (though it's certainly not a bad idea, if you can work it out), but I often wonder if the benefits of our Lenten spiritual disciplines are sometimes lost by our Easter laxity. Lent, after all, is only six weeks long, while the liturgical season of Easter lasts for eight weeks. What would happen if we lived the Easter season with as much fervor as we live Lent? This question gives us a chance to reflect on this.

The Color of Easter

Every liturgical season has its color—both physically (as in violet for Lent and white for Easter, as shown in the sacred vestments used for Mass), but also spiritually. Trying to echo in our own spiritual lives the color of the seasons is a wise practice.

The color of Easter is joy, the joy of definitive victory. Christ has taken all sin and evil into his own soul, in a sense, and done away with it. God's mercy has shown itself infinitely stronger than the devil's poison. This is the message so beautifully expressed in the Easter Sequence, sung before the Gospel is read for the Mass of Our Lord's Resurrection.

What can we do to color our spiritual lives with Easter joy? Here are three suggestions that can help make this season fruitful for growing in holiness.

Stay connected to the liturgy. The readings for daily Mass during Easter take us on an exciting journey through the Last Supper discourse and the amazing and frightening experience of the early Church. We should spend time reading commentaries about these biblical passages, meditating on them, and allowing God to speak to our hearts through them. The main message of the liturgical readings throughout Easter is that Christ is still among us, even after his passion, resurrection, and ascension, and he is present precisely through his Church. I always find it deeply encouraging to read a book or two about the history of the Church or the life of a saint during Easter. It reminds me that my own Christian journey is a part of a much bigger story, that I am not alone in my defeats and victories.

Find ways to rejoice. This time of year tends to be quite busy—especially for those with kids in school. Make a point of doing some things that you enjoy. Just as in Lent denying ourselves some legitimate delights is a way to unite ourselves to Christ's self-sacrifice, so during Easter we should intentionally enjoy the good things of life as a way to unite ourselves to Christ's victory and triumph. There is always a victory celebration when one's team wins the championship. Jesus has won the eternal championship, and we are on his team; we need to celebrate that!

Obviously, I am not suggesting that you dive into sinful pleasures or overindulge in self-centered activities. But I am recommending that you intentionally look for ways to rejoice, to enjoy God's goodness such that joy overflows from your spirit, into your emotions, and even into your body. Why not make Sunday lunch a truly festive occasion for your family and friends every Sunday of the Easter season? Different family members can take turns being in charge of the menu each week. Why not make a special trip or two to your favorite museum or take some extra time to enjoy your favorite music or a favorite author? Why not carve out some extra time during Easter for your whole family, or at least a few of you, to enjoy some activities that you haven't had a chance to do for a long time? Why not tastefully reflect Easter joy in the way you dress when you go to work? If we surround these activities with a spiritual and prayerful intention to celebrate Christ's victory, they become means of worship. God rejoices to see his children rejoice.

Reach out. The Bible teaches us that "it is more blessed to give than to receive" (Acts 20:35). Like the candlelight service during the Easter Vigil, we can share with others the light of Christ's victory that we have received and roll back the tattered shadows of the kingdom of darkness. Renewing our efforts to bring others closer to Christ and help others who are in need—both those close to us and those far away—can color our lives with Easter joy, if we season those efforts with prayer and faith. Christians should smile more during Easter, because true joy draws forth joy.

HOW CAN I PREPARE WELL FOR ADVENT?

It's great to ask this question before Advent arrives! That stress and tension does not come from the Holy Spirit. So, how to make it a meaningful Advent? I would like to offer five suggestions.

First, decide what you are going to say no to. The Advent and Christmas seasons get filled up with a lot of stuff. We end up rushing around so much—parties, visits with relatives and friends, family reunions, kids back from college, shopping, school concerts, vacation, service projects, parish activities... To stay spiritually grounded during these weeks of intense activity requires planning ahead. It didn't used to require as much as it does now, by the way. In times past, local customs defined how families and communities spent their time. Today, however, we have so many options that we end up overcommitting ourselves and going 100 mph. It's hard to pray in that scenario. It's hard to reflect and enjoy God's gifts. It's easy to become self-absorbed and superficial.

The remedy? Well, as mundane as it may sound, we have to apply basic time-management techniques. Sit down with your spouse (or maybe with the whole family) sometime before Thanksgiving, and look at the calendar. Identify the commitments you must fulfill and the ones that you really want to commit to. Consciously, intentionally decide to make those truly meaningful. (In going over your calendar, think about including some of the items mentioned below.) Then consciously, intentionally decide to say no to other things that come up on the spur of the moment—or at least don't say yes to them right away until you can talk it over with your spouse. This will give you a measure of interior peace right from the start; you won't be at the mercy of the apparently urgent tugs that are sure to come. And you won't end up at the last minute trying to squeeze all the important things into three or four days of frantic activity. You will have planned ahead. Remember, peace is the tranquility that comes from order (according to St. Augustine).

Second, change your meditation material. I'm assuming that you have a daily God-time in which you engage in personal prayer and Christian meditation. If you don't—start! If you do, think about changing the source you are using for your meditation. If you have been meditating on the daily liturgy, for example, think about switching to a devotional book of some sort (for example, you could simply meditate on the Gospel of St. Luke from start to finish, using the commentaries in a resource like my book *The Better Part,* one unit per day). If you have been using a favorite devotional, switch to the liturgy, or to another devotional (Alban Goodier's classic *The Prince of Peace* is wonderful, if you can find a copy). The liturgical seasons are given to us precisely because we need to change things up. We are creatures with one foot in time and another in eternity. This means we need rhythms in our lives, and rhythm means some things stay the same (Advent comes every year), but some things change (Advent doesn't last all year). This needs to be reflected in our spiritual disciplines.

Third, plug into your parish. Every parish has Advent and Christmas liturgies (like the daily Mass liturgies and the Advent penitential services), and they also have other seasonal activities (like Christian service projects). Engaging in them as a family, if possible, will help you keep Christ in the center, and you will also help others to keep Christ in the center. Building up your parish by participating in these liturgies and activities is a specific, nitty-gritty way to build up the kingdom of Christ on earth. Personally, I would love to see as many parishioners going to daily Mass during Advent as we see during Lent.

Fourth, do an Advent retreat. This could be a weekend retreat, a retreat organized in your diocese or offered by a local retreat center, or just a simple personal retreat that you do during a full day or half-day in a quiet place away from the ordinary hustle and bustle, like a convent or a monastery. We need silence and reflection in our lives, and even a daily God-time, lived with devotion and dedication, needs to be bolstered once in a while with extended periods of silence and prayer. Bring some good spiritual reading on your retreat, and maybe work in some extra time for more-than-usual spiritual reading throughout Advent. A worthy spiritual reading project would be to download from the Vatican website the Midnight Mass homilies of Benedict XVI and those of John Paul II. (He gave twenty-six of them!) Make a booklet out of them and work through them little by little.

Fifth, choose your entertainment strategically. We all benefit from the inspiration and relaxation that entertainment affords us. We actually need to make healthy recreation a part of our lives—we are not robots, after all. But too often we aren't strategic about this; we just kind of do whatever everyone else does, or whatever we have always done. Take some time to reflect, individually and as a family, on what entertainment activities you will enjoy during Advent and Christmas. Maybe you will want to fast from a particular activity during Advent (remember, it is a penitential season). Maybe you will want to schedule some sledding adventures—with lots of hot cocoa when you come home! Or maybe you will simply want to watch your four favorite Christmas movies together as a family (maybe inviting friends to join you) on the Saturdays before each of the four Sundays of Advent, with lots of fresh popcorn. *It's a Wonderful Life,* for example, is a powerful film that can provide necessary relaxation and also spiritual inspiration.

In addition to these five suggestions, it's important to remember that the primary agent in experiencing a spiritually fruitful Advent is God. We can make adjustments and do our best to have our activities reflect our true priorities, but in the end, God is the one most interested in using this liturgical season to draw us closer to himself, to fill us with more of his wisdom, and to give us new tastes of supernatural joy. He will draw us and guide us and inspire us if we follow his lead.

IS IT OKAY TO RELAX MY SPIRITUAL PRACTICES DURING A VACATION?

This is an important question. We live in an almost completely secularized popular culture in which the highest good (as habitually presented by advertising and entertainment) is enjoyment. And so, living for the weekends, for vacation, for retirement is constantly offered to us as the proper priority in life. Even though, as active Catholics, our friendship with Christ has given us a different set of priorities, the bombardment of secular images and messages we navigate through each day has its effect. By reflecting briefly on a truly Christian view of vacation, we can, I hope, exterminate some well-disguised mental parasites that tend to disturb our interior peace.

As usual, the best place to start is at the end. What is the goal of a rule of life (sometimes referred to as a program of life)? What is the purpose of vacation? Answering those questions will pave the way to an answer to your more specific question about how to adjust one's rule of life during vacation.

The Purpose of a Rule of Life

A rule of life, with its prayer commitments and plan for spiritual growth, is your own personal mission statement. It provides you with some specific parameters to help you stay on track and continuously grow in your love for Christ and use your talents to further his kingdom. In other words, your rule of life is a designed to keep you focused on what matters most.

The Purpose of Vacation

What is the purpose of vacation? A good analogy comes from farming. Before planting a new crop, a farmer plows and fertilizes his field. He has to turn over the earth, expose it to the air, break up the hard surface, turn over the roots and stalks left over from the last harvest, and refresh the soil under the surface by exposing it to the air, sun, and rain. Then he is ready to plant a new crop.

Vacation does something similar for our souls. Daily life in this fallen world is demanding, exhausting. We pour mental, psychological, spiritual, and emotional energy into work, the duties of our state in life, and relationships. Our activity drains the nutrients from the soil of our human nature, drying it out. Vacation is met to refresh that soil, reinvigorating it and restoring balance to our physical and psychological organism. Thus restored, we can return to the demands of our life mission with renewed energy and determination. An annual vacation is to each year what a day off is to each week. As Benedict XVI put it: "I hope everyone, especially those in greatest need, will be able to take a bit of vacation to restore their physical and spiritual energy and recover a healthy contact with nature" (Angelus, July 8, 2007).

In short, we go on vacation from what we do, not from who we are.

Vacation is meant to provide necessary rest from and rejuvenation for the normal, meaningful, but draining activities of daily life; it is not meant to separate us from God or be a pause on our journey toward deeper communion with him. Vacation must never be an excuse to pray less, to skip out on the sacraments, to indulge in irresponsibility, or to flirt with occasions of sin. In that sense, a rule of life retains full validity during periods of vacation. And remember that your companions and circumstances will not be perfect even while you are on vacation; you will still need to exercise self-sacrifice, patience, and other virtues (especially those you most need to develop). If you expect and accept this, it won't spoil your rest. After all, as our Lord reminded us, "there is more joy in giving than receiving" (Acts 20:35).

On the other hand, a vacation will yield little rest and rejuvenation if it fails to include a notable change from the daily grind—the soil has to be plowed in order to be refreshed. And this change can certainly be reflected in some of the more external aspects even of our spiritual lives. Here are some examples that may help illustrate the point. They can apply to weekly days off as well as annual vacation periods.

Some Practical Suggestions

1. If your family or spouse is not in the same place as you are regarding your faith, try not to fret about it. God knows the situation, and he knows the limits that puts on your own activities. He sees your heart, and he will provide chances for you to have the faith experiences and times of silence and prayer you would really like to plan into your vacation schedule.

2. If you normally do your morning meditation in your room or in a chapel, you may want to do it outside, walking through a beautiful natural setting. If you normally pray your rosary in your car on the way to work, you may want to take the time to pray it while walking through a park or sitting quietly in a church.

3. Change the times of day during which you do your normal prayer commitments. If you usually rise early for your prayer time, perhaps you'll want to switch to mid-afternoon or sometime in the evening.

4. Use different source material for your daily meditation, changing up the themes that you reflect and pray about. For example, if you usually

meditate on the daily Gospel, during vacation you may want to find a good commentary on a book of the Old Testament or one of the epistles, and meditate on that instead.

5. Put on hold whatever books or materials you are using for spiritual reading or faith study. For vacation, change gears. Take something fresh, something that really attracts you, maybe something you always wanted to read but never had time to (a historical novel, an old favorite, a classic). Of course, it should be edifying and inspiring, not scandalous or superficial.

6. Live Sundays the way you would always like to live them during the year—totally dedicated to God and family. As Pope Benedict put it:

> In periods of work, with its frenetic pace, and in holiday periods we must reserve moments for God. We must open our lives to him, addressing to him a thought, a reflection, a brief prayer, and above all we must not forget Sunday as the Lord's Day, the day of the Liturgy, in order to perceive God's beauty itself in the beauty of our churches, in our sacred music and in the word of God, letting him enter our being. Only in this way does our life become great, become true life.[4]

7. It can be nice to include a visit, or even a mini-pilgrimage, to a shrine or a notable sacred location. But you'll want to make sure this is fun for the whole family or group. If no one else is interested, you may want to take a solo trip.

8. Give yourself a motto for the vacation. Most people following a rule of life have a motto that sums up and unifies their spiritual work. It can be useful to give yourself a motto for vacation, something that will help remind you of your purpose for this time—such as, "Let not your hearts be troubled" (John 14:1).

In general, be flexible with the externals of your spiritual life but faithful to the substance.

Some General Ideas

If at all possible, a change of place is beneficial. I know of two families that simply trade houses for two weeks each summer. This is less expensive than going to a vacation resort, but it still provided the change of atmosphere that is so helpful for healthy rest. If you really can't afford to go somewhere, at least change the places where you do your normal activities. Eat outside, for example, instead of in the dining room.

Change gears on the type of activity you engage in. Someone who works in an office, for example, should be sure to spend time outside and enjoy some physical activity; someone who works outside should think about ways to engage in culturally enriching vacation activities. Divide up the necessary chores in a different way than you normally do.

Unplug as much as possible from your cell phone, email, and other electronic media that are an integral part of your normal daily activity. This may seem impossible, but it isn't—really! It just requires determination and planning ahead. I guarantee that if you do this, you won't regret it. Along the same lines, plan ahead regarding the amount and kind of media entertainment you will use during vacation.

Include simple ways of playing and engaging in friendly competition in your vacation activities. Consider board games like Scrabble or Pictionary, cards, or sports and outdoor games that everyone can enjoy (beanbag toss, badminton, volleyball).

Make a point of having regular and abundant contact with nature. Walk, sit in the sun, enjoy the sunset—enjoy the natural surroundings wherever you go.

Sleep well and eat fresh food whenever possible. Your vacation should provide nourishing rest and refreshment.

Know what type of activity helps you relax, and make time for it. Some people relax more by being alone, reading, and reflecting. Others relax more through social interaction or physical activity. We each have to lovingly help those around us relax, but we do that better if we are also finding time to relax ourselves.

WHY DO THE SAINTS CAUTION AGAINST EXCESSIVE CURIOSITY?

Your question raises a crucial issue for spiritual growth in general, and especially for spiritual growth in the digital world.

As we all know, the digital revolution has also spawned an information revolution. Today, our fingertips have immediate access to more information than world scholars could have gathered in an entire lifetime just a couple hundred years ago. As with all technological advancements, the digital revolution is morally neutral. Our increased access to information can either aid our pursuit of holiness or hinder it. It makes the virtue of learning easier to develop, but it also makes the vice of curiosity easier to fall in to. That's the key distinction for answering your question: learning vs. curiosity.

The Virtue of Studiositas

We cannot love what we do not know. Studying God's creation can help us know God better, just as studying the works of an artist can help know an artist better, and by knowing God better we can love him better— which is the purpose of our existence. Our intelligence is meant for this, in fact. That's why the Christian spiritual tradition catalogues *studiositas* as a virtue—"the virtue of study," of applying our minds to learning, so that we can grow in knowledge and understanding of the world, ourselves, and God.

In modern times, we tend to use the word *study* to refer strictly to academic activity, with an unpleasant connotation. But the traditional virtue of *studiositas* is broader. It refers to the zeal required to really learn, the effort to understand things, the application of one's mind to the task of growing in knowledge and wisdom. *Learning* may be a better modern equivalent of the Latin *studiositas* in this context.

The Vice of Curiositas

But like every power of the human soul, this capacity to learn can be deformed. Instead of applying ourselves to develop the virtue of study, we can fall into the vice of *curiositas,* or curiosity. In the Christian spiritual tradition, this word, like *studiositas,* has a technical meaning. The vice of curiosity refers to the superficial gathering of information, the thirst to imbibe the latest headline or rumor just because it's new. Curiosity stops where learning begins. It's like the butterfly that flits from flower to flower without gathering any nectar, whereas the bee will settle into a flower and drink up, taking time to gather all that the flower has to offer. Curiosity is often associated with other vices—gossip especially, but also inordinate attachment to fads and fashions, wasting time, and tale-bearing (vying to be the first to pass along juicy rumors).

Curiosity in this sense of superficial thirst for new and titillating information impedes spiritual growth. God is always speaking to us, but if we are constantly bopping around and chatterboxing, we make it hard for ourselves to hear him. We tend not to take the necessary time for reflection and self-analysis. We are so caught up in the exterior aspect of events, whether those in our own lives or in the world around us, that we rarely pause to consider the interior aspects: causes and consequences, meanings and implications.

God rarely shouts. He loves us too much to force us to hear him. Jesus refused to jump off the pinnacle of the Temple to get people's attention, even though that certainly would have made the headlines. He addresses us more intimately, more quietly, more personally. The vice of curiosity, or superficiality, makes our souls hard and impenetrable to his advances, like the hardened dirt path where some of the seed fell in the parable of the sower, so that his words don't permeate and take root. Instead, the birds (the devil) come and snatch them away by keeping us "distracted from distractions by distractions," as T.S. Eliot once put it.[5]

Intellectual Greed

Another vice can deform our God-given capacity to learn: greed. Usually we associate greed with money. But we can also be greedy when it comes to knowledge. Greed is an inordinate desire for possessions, and knowledge is a spiritual possession. Intellectual greediness differs from curiosity in the sense that it usually involves deeper knowledge. But it also impedes our spiritual growth.

On the one hand, as we grow in knowledge, we can become snobbish, looking down at others for not knowing as much as we do. This is a direct affront to Christian charity.

On the other hand, it also can keep us distracted. In this case, the thirst to have new experiences and develop new areas of expertise is inordinate, out of proportion to our mission in life. The enjoyment of acquiring new knowledge, which is legitimate in itself, becomes so all-consuming that the duties of one's state in life are neglected. I have known more than one marriage that crashed because a scholarly spouse became as overly obsessed with research as greedy businessmen do with making money.

This can even happen with knowledge of spiritual things. Growing in the knowledge of God and his plan for our lives should never disconnect a man from his wife and children, for example. Knowledge is meant to be at the service of love, and in the end we will be judged on how we loved God by fulfilling his will, not on how much we knew about Church teaching and the lives of the saints.

HOW CAN I BALANCE BEING WITH DOING?

There comes a point in our spiritual life where God invites us to another level, a deeper level of intimacy and integration. We begin to yearn for our many good actions and activities to flow more directly from our intimate experience of God's love and goodness. Instead of having two parallel buckets in your life (intimacy *with* God; activities *for* God), we become drawn toward a more integrated reality. We sense that our active life should be more of an overflow of our contemplative life—like a fountain with two levels, the top level filling up and overflowing into the bottom level, which in turn fills up and overflows. God is interested in something besides what we do—he wants more of our hearts, more of who we are: "Give me your heart" (Proverbs 23:26).

As you deepen the contemplative dimension of your life, and connect more integrally to the active dimension of your life, you will be surprised at the results. Instead of finding yourself tired out (whether physically, psychologically, or both) by all your activity, your energy level will stay strong. Instead of being less productive, you will actually bear much more supernatural fruit than you could ever have imagined. This is logical. As God's grace—God himself present and at work in our souls—becomes the primary agent of all we do, he is more readily able to compensate for all our natural limitations. This is why the lives of the saints show such a disproportionate ratio of activity to fruitfulness. Giving more space to God's grace allows our contribution to his kingdom to increase exponentially, though it may not always be visible.

Here are five ways you can integrate your activities for God and your intimacy with God:

1. Escape with the Lord. You need to create space in your life where you can unplug and hear God's voice. Get in the habit of going on retreats. Taking half a day every month and a full weekend or four days every year or every six months to be alone with the Lord will help immensely. Our lives are noisy. They are busy. That's the world we live in. We have to intentionally slow down on a regular basis. You can do some of these retreats on your own, but as a rule, it's better to go on a directed retreat. You can explore what retreat centers have to offer or look for monthly mornings or evenings of reflection in your area. The key is that the retreats should have plenty of silence built in to them. Even if it involves traveling, it's beneficial to go on retreats regularly.

2. Schedule Daily Chats. Mental prayer (Christian meditation) should become part of your daily routine. If you are already doing this, you need to go deeper. If at all possible, increase the amount of time you dedicate to it. Mental prayer is a privileged spiritual exercise. It gives the Holy Spirit room to personalize the truths of our faith, to apply them to your particular life and circumstances. There is no substitute for it. Growing in mental prayer enhances our vocal prayer and our liturgical prayer. It's the secret weapon for consistent spiritual growth.

3. Don't Be a Lone Ranger. I highly recommend spiritual direction. It can be challenging to find a spiritual director, but it is possible and the rewards are great. God just likes to work in our lives through other human beings. This is his methodology. If you ask God to provide you with a spiritual director and make a reasonable effort to find one, he won't keep you waiting too long (or if he does, he will supply some kind of substitute).

4. Bathe Your Mind. Spiritual reading fills your mind with light. It consists of regular reading of solid books that explain what it means to be a Catholic Christian. When I say regular, I mean reading for fifteen or twenty minutes every day. Read about the great, wonderful reality of who we are as adopted children of God. Read about the experiences of our older brothers and sisters in the faith—the lives of the saints. Read solid guidance about how to grow in prayer, in virtue, in intimacy with God. Read about God himself—commentaries on Scripture and on the truths of our faith.

Every day, our minds are bombarded with ideas and images that contradict, subtly or not so subtly, our Catholic worldview. We need to intentionally counteract this secular tsunami. You don't have to finish every book you start. Just make the effort, and you will start finding books that really resonate, and these will provide the Holy Spirit more opportunities to instruct and illuminate your mind and heart. As much I am a fan of the Internet, reading posts online is not the same as reading whole books. Books go deeper. They give you more to mull over, more to meditate on. Our minds and hearts need time to digest the amazing truths of our faith; reading books helps give us that time.

5. *Live Your Life in God's Time.* Start treating Sundays and the liturgical seasons the way you know you should but never have been able to so far. Live the Lord's Day as the Lord's Day, not just the last day of the weekend. Live the liturgical seasons and feasts, preparing for them, decorating the house for them, preparing special meals for them. It's not really a question of slowing down the pace of your life—you want to *Christify* it. You need to gradually transition your life so that your external activities, your family life and friendships, and above all your own mind and heart, are following the rhythms of God's time, and that's the liturgical year. Our society doesn't do this and never has, at least not in our lifetime. Because of this, we have no concept of the difference it can make when we govern our time by God's time, instead of trying to squeeze time for God into our secular schedules. I know this is hard. It seems impossible to live Sunday well without frenetic activity. But believe me, living Sunday well is the first and necessary step to re-dimensioning the frenetic activity.

By incorporating these five things into your life, you can begin a new chapter in your spiritual life. If it seems overwhelming, don't fret! Just identify one step you can take to begin and take it. Then identify one more step and take it. You don't have to implement them all over night. Recognize that the Holy Spirit at work in your heart, drawing closer to you, and calling you to seek him more ardently, to know him more intimately, and to love him more passionately.

IS IT POSSIBLE TO BE TOO SPIRITUAL
OR PASSIONATE ABOUT MY FAITH?

Sometimes the people around us can help identify imbalances in our lives to which we ourselves are oblivious. We have all experienced this. Just think about friends who make unfortunate dating choices: they put themselves in relationships that wear them down instead of build them up, but they don't seem to see it. So, if someone is consistently receiving feedback that he or she has gone overboard in piety from people he or she knows and respects, the first reaction should be to do some self-reflection: "Is my life of piety somehow turning people away from Christ?" In this context, I offer four possible self-examination questions:

1. Am I able to carry on a friendly and interesting conversation with people—friends, acquaintances, strangers—about nonreligious topics?

The answer should be yes. A mature Christian should have a lively interest in simply being human. Think about St. John Paul II and how he so easily met people where they were at. He enjoyed skiing and soccer; he enjoyed movies and art. Benedict XVI plays Mozart to relax. St. John Bosco performed magic tricks for kids. St. Gianna Beretta Molla kept up on fashion trends. We, too, should have healthy interests and hobbies that are simply human, not directly related to our piety (though they must never interfere with our friendship with Christ). Christians should be interesting people, enjoyable to be around, welcome in any kind of setting, able to connect with people where they are at.

2. Do I regularly have a hidden agenda in my conversations with other people?

We have to be really careful here. As Christ's ambassadors, it is up to us to bear witness to his truth and love, especially to those who do not know or accept God's truth and love. But as we grow in our own love for God and his Church, a subtle temptation to pride can seep into our relationships. We can start thinking that we know exactly what other people need, and so we start manipulating them—saying one thing and meaning another, or trying to pressure them (instead of motivating them) into doing what's right. This is a false kind of charity. Only God knows the whole story of a human heart. We are not saviors; we are just witnesses and messengers.

Certainly we can be creative and energetic in finding ways to communicate Christ's message, but we need to have an absolute respect for every person, treating them like people, not like pet projects. Otherwise, we end up seeking our own glory instead of God's glory. This balance can sometimes be hard to maintain. It takes a lot of prayer and a lot of humility. We are just instruments of the Holy Spirit, junior partners; he is the one in charge. As a rule of thumb, we should make a decent and responsible effort to share with others what God has given to us, but not force it down their throats. We are to love our neighbors as ourselves, respecting them, helping them, and building them up, not belittling them or riding roughshod over them.

3. Do I lead a balanced lifestyle, in accordance with the duties of my state in life?

The touchstone of our walk with Christ is God's will. Jesus's own rule of life was: "I can do nothing on my own authority…but [I do] the will of him who sent me" (John 5:30). We find God's will in the commandments of the Bible and the Church, in the example of Christ, in the duties of our state in life, and in the inspirations of the Holy Spirit (which will never contradict the first three).

If you are a single professional, for example, you should work hard, be engaged in your parish, pursue healthy hobbies, participate in an active social life, and most importantly, have a regular and substantial prayer life. If you are married with children, the commitment to your husband and kids will necessarily diminish the amount of time and energy you can dedicate to your profession, hobbies, and social life, but those aspects of normal humanhood should not disappear. If your life of piety consistently crowds everything else out, it may be a sign that you have a religious vocation—but not if you're already married! Jesus was clear when he said, "Let your light so shine before men, that they may see your good works and give glory to your Father who is in heaven" (Matthew 5:16). If you are spending all of your time in church, how can that happen?

4. Do I cling to friendships or hobbies that habitually put me in occasions of sin?

This is a key point. We can sometimes use the "let your light shine" commandment as an excuse to stay too heavily involved in fashionable or pleasurable social circles that are actually riddled with sinful behavior. I remember guys in college who used to engage in what they called "missionary dating." They would date girls who did not share a Christian worldview or Christian morals, telling themselves that by dating these girls they would help convert them. The opposite always happened.

As adults, we can fall into the same trap. The businessman or lawyer who convinces himself that he has to go to the strip club after work in order to build a relationship with a potential client is not "letting his light shine"; he is exposing it to a wind that may blow it out. The socially active Catholic woman who keeps on lunching at the country club with friends who regularly spend the whole lunch gossiping is impeding her spiritual progress and giving sin a foothold. We have to invest quality time in friendships that are healthy, and at least in some friendships in which our core Christian values (the pursuit of holiness) are shared.

On the other hand, this doesn't mean that we are supposed to isolate ourselves from all contact with secular people. Avoiding habitual gossip sessions at the country club doesn't mean you can't have lunch or tennis with a friend or two who don't share your faith or worldview. Not at all! Answering Christ's call to be "the salt of the earth" (Matthew 5:13) requires being in the world. But we have to avoid being of the world; when socializing starts causing our salt to lose its taste, we are doing no one any favors.

Reflecting on these four questions may help you identify if you are out of balance. If so, you may indeed be turning people away from Christ. But if you are pretty much balanced (we are never perfectly balanced, and we constantly have to adjust in order to keep even our imperfect balance), then you simply need to keep forging ahead, trusting that any "sign of contradiction" (see Luke 2:34) will be used by God, somehow, to draw others closer to him.

In the Face of Opposition

Second, we need to remember that whenever we are truly seeking to follow Christ, we will inevitably face misunderstanding, opposition, and even persecution. This is just the way it is. Jesus was really clear about it: "If you were of the world, the world would love its own; but because you are not of the world, but I chose you out of the world, therefore the world hates you" (John 15:19).

This opposition can be painful and confusing. It is more hurtful when it comes from those closest to us—a disdainful spouse, for example, or a fellow Catholic parishioner who resents the call to conscience that our example makes to them. We must not let this kind of opposition interfere with our quest for holiness. Rather, we have to refrain from judging these critics (we can't see their whole heart), and keep our eye on the ball: loving God with all our heart, soul, mind, and strength, and loving our neighbor as ourselves.

WHAT ABOUT STAY-AT-HOME MOMS VERSUS WORKING MOTHERS?

Many women feel strongly about this issue, for a lot of reasons. One weighty factor is the way motherhood has been deprecated, systematically and violently, in modern American culture. During the last thirty years, a false feminism that equates a woman's success as a woman with outperforming men in the professional career-derby has been reinforced by TV, movies, novels, magazines, and legal trends. As a result, many women of faith who still perceive the value and beauty of motherhood automatically tend to associate following a professional career with following that false, destructive, feminism. Likewise, many women who have imbibed some of the false feminism can feel threatened when they meet happy stay-at-home moms.

Keep First Things First

Church teaching in this area can help foster a more balanced view. Every married couple's primary vocation is their marriage. Their spousal relationship is actually a sacrament, a sign and agent of God's grace in the world. And so, striving with God's help to build a family that truly is a domestic church, a school of Christian virtue, a reflection of the goodness and active love of the Trinity, and a training ground for holiness is a wife and mother's main mission in life. Anyone, husband or wife, who lets merely self-centered desires inhibit the pursuit of that mission is deviating from God's marvelous plan. Company presidents who regularly work eighty-hour weeks just to climb the corporate ladder, to the detriment of their relationships at home, are falling into idolatry. (They are also making themselves miserable, because achievements can never fill up our hearts, which were created to love and be loved.) The same goes for the hobbyists or socialites who neglect family life in order to have more time to indulge their passions and vanity.

No Family Is an Island

The domestic church is not meant to be an island, however, just as no Christian is meant to be cut off from the mission of evangelizing the world. We are all called to spread Christ's grace, to actively build up a civilization of justice and love. Children of stay-at-home moms learn this when they see their parents engaging in the world beyond their four walls. Even stay-at-home moms need to be reaching out to neighbors, to other families, to the parish, to the community—they are meant to share their gifts with those outside their immediate family. In this way, they become living example of what it means to be a missionary, a messenger of God's goodness and grace, since every follower of Christ is by nature exactly that. By plugging into the wider community (and involving the kids in those efforts when possible), children learn that they aren't the center of the universe. Rather, they are part of a family that has a mission to build up the Church and build a better world.

Get Practical

If a woman desires to put her professional skills back to work outside the home, it very well could come from the Lord. It's a good idea to keep a personal journal of these thoughts, dreams, and hopes. Start reflecting on whether they are rooted in a vain desire to get some recognition from peers and professionals (instead of just toddlers), or if they are truly rooted in a joy-filled desire to better the Church and the world with the gifts God has given you. If the motivation is Christian and not selfish (you may need the help of a spiritual director or a very honest friend to discern this), then take some initial steps to find out how you can go in that direction without neglecting your primary vocation (you may need to get creative to balance the two).

WHAT'S THE BEST WAY TO DEAL WITH BORING HOMILIES?

As a convert to Catholicism, I have experienced the dynamic, courageous, real, and relevant presentation of Scripture so common in the newer evangelical churches. And I've also experienced some disappointment when I discovered that many Catholic homilies don't have the same sparkle. Here are four suggestions that address this question.

First, don't stop eating. First, search for spiritual nourishment in other places. Evangelicals are trained to expect the main spiritual meal to come from the Sunday sermon. It is the centerpiece of Protestant worship, after all. It is not the same for us Catholics, but that doesn't mean we have to go without! You can feed your soul with profound, enriching, exciting, and transforming Catholic teaching from many sources besides the Sunday homily. In fact, once you begin to discover the richness within the Catholic heritage, you really won't miss the rousing evangelical sermons much at all.

We all need to keep seeking a deeper knowledge of our faith. Supplement what you hear on Sundays with other sources. If you like to read, you can discover an entire universe of Catholic books. If you learn better by listening, I highly recommend listening to audio books or other inspiring recordings available. There are many sources that can keep your mind and heart engaged as you continue this new season in your spiritual journey. And if you can engage in this ongoing formation in the company of like-minded folks, all the better!

Second, listen to homilies from God's perspective. Don't tune out the homilies; instead adjust your expectations. Remember, the homily is actually part of the sacred liturgy. Only an ordained minister can preach a homily. It's connected to the sacrament of holy orders. If you approach it from this supernatural perspective, you can be certain that the Holy Spirit will give you something in the homily, even if the priest or deacon didn't have time to do their homework or doesn't have a natural flare for preaching. On her deathbed, St. Elizabeth of Hungary replayed and talked about all the spiritual insights she had received through listening to homilies (there were far fewer books available to a young noblewoman back in the fourteenth century than then there are today). I am sure the preachers were not all at the A-plus level, yet she had approached the homilies knowing that God *wanted* to communicate something to her soul through them, and so she focused more on listening to the Holy Spirit than on identifying the rhetorical weaknesses. We all need to do the same. It's a powerful way to exercise our faith in the Church and the sacraments.

Third, curb your frustration through exercising patience. The enemy of your soul would love to turn this issue into a constant, looming distraction. You don't have to let that happen. Remember: "Blessed are the merciful, for they shall obtain mercy" (Matthew 5:7). Exercise mercy toward the homilist. Trust that God can make him a saint regardless of his homiletic performance. Trust that God loves him, and that he loves God (why else would he continue on as a priest in today's world?). Trust that God can work miracles through broken instruments. You don't have to pretend that a bad homily is a good homily. But why not focus your attention more on how you can serve and support the parish than on aspects of parish life that you can hardly influence at all? In short, we all need to learn to "let the peace of Christ rule in [our] hearts" (Colossians 3:15), even in the face of negligence, imperfections, and problems. Striving for that ideal gives great glory to God, because it requires the exercise of supernatural trust. (Of course, if the homilies you hear are blatantly heretical and truly destructive, you need to take action. Talk directly to your priest or deacon about your concerns. If that doesn't help, you may need to inform your bishop, through his diocesan assistant for priestly life.)

Fourth, remember that intellectual formation is only one part of integral spiritual growth. Prayer, active love, faithfulness to God's will, and character development are also essential aspects along the path to spiritual maturity. Perhaps in this season of your journey, our Lord is inviting you to focus more on one or more of those than on the intellectual part. I am not advocating ignorant Catholicism, but rather integral formation, becoming a fully mature Catholic. As Thomas á Kempis put it so wonderfully five hundred years ago, "I would rather feel contrition than know how to define it."[6]

Chapter Five

Catholicism

EVERY SUNDAY, CATHOLICS THROUGHOUT THE world go to Mass. In the first part of the celebration, we listen to readings from the Bible and then to a homily explaining those readings and applying them to our lives. After the homily, we all pray the Creed, reaffirming our belief in the Catholic faith. One of the phrases of the Creed states: "I believe in one, holy, Catholic and apostolic Church." One Church. What does that mean? In any given town there are a whole bunch of churches: Methodist, Baptist, Episcopalian, Evangelical. How do we reconcile this apparent contradiction: that we believe in one Church, but even while we're professing that faith a dozen other churches are having services of their own just down the road? What makes our Catholic faith different?

In this final chapter, we'll examine some of the differences between Catholicism and other faiths, and we'll look at some of the things that are unique to being Catholic.

WHY IS IT IMPORTANT TO ATTEND SUNDAY MASS?

Attending Sunday Mass (on Sunday or on the vigil) and Mass on Holy Days of Obligation is a primary responsibility of every Catholic. The *Catechism* teaches:

> The precept of the Church specifies the law of the Lord more precisely: "On Sundays and other holy days of obligation the faithful are bound to participate in the Mass." "The precept

of participating in the Mass is satisfied by assistance at a Mass which is celebrated anywhere in a Catholic rite either on the holy day or on the evening of the preceding day."

The Sunday Eucharist is the foundation and confirmation of all Christian practice. For this reason the faithful are obliged to participate in the Eucharist on days of obligation, unless excused for a serious reason (for example, illness, the care of infants) or dispensed by their own pastor. Those who deliberately fail in this obligation commit a grave sin. (*CCC* 2180–2181)

On the website of the United States Conference of Catholic Bishops (USCCB), there is a report from the bishops' *Catechism* committee that correlates extensively quotations from John Paul II's 1998 Apostolic Letter, *Dies Domini,* and various numbers from the *Catechism.* Reading through the correlation is a fantastic way to meditate on the reasons behind the Sunday obligation. Here is one of the paragraphs from *Dies Domini* that the bishops' committee cites—its language is a bit technical but still quite clear:

> Even if in the earliest times it was not judged necessary to be prescriptive, the church has not ceased to confirm this obligation of conscience, which rises from the inner need felt so strongly by the Christians of the first centuries. It was only later, faced with the halfheartedness or negligence of some, that the church had to make explicit the duty to attend Sunday Mass: More often than not this was done in the form of exhortation, but at times the church had to resort to specific canonical precepts.... The present code reiterates this, saying that "on Sundays and other Holy Days of obligation, the faithful are bound to attend Mass." This legislation has normally been understood as entailing a grave obligation: This is the teaching of the *Catechism of the Catholic Church,* and it is easy to understand why if we keep in mind how vital Sunday is for the Christian life.[7]

In the USCCB's own *Catechism for Adults*, they emphasize the importance of Sunday Mass attendance: "God, through the Church, obliges us to make Sunday holy by participation in the Eucharist and by our being prayerfully reflective as far as possible."[8]

"Judge Not, that You Be Not Judged" (Matthew 7:1)

From the above, it's clear that the Sunday Eucharist is not optional, and that purposely snubbing God by skipping Mass is indeed a grave sin. But remember, we are not called to judge our neighbors. We have to avoid falling into self-righteous Pharisaism in the face of Catholics who do not fulfill this responsibility. Instead of condemning them, we should reach out to them, help them to understand the many reasons behind this duty, and the many positive fruits that come from fulfilling it. This means that we ourselves need to understand those reasons and live Sunday well enough to begin experiencing some of those fruits.

Common Sense and Pastoral Sensitivity

John Paul II's apostolic letter on this topic did address some challenges to living Sunday well that we face in these postmodern times. Basically, the issue has to do with working on Sundays. Our world no longer universally recognizes Sunday as the Lord's Day. As a result, many Catholics, in order to keep their jobs, sometimes have to work on Sundays. Likewise, for those of us who do try to live the Lord's Day well, some family and recreational activities that are perfectly in synch with the Sunday rest require *other* people to work—at restaurants, for instance.

This challenge was one reason the Second Vatican Council authorized the vigil Mass (Mass on Saturday evening) to fulfill the Sunday obligation. Additionally, if a Catholic simply cannot make any of the Sunday Masses, he can speak with his local pastor to receive a dispensation from this obligation and work out alternative solutions.

Regarding working on a day that is meant to be for rest, the *Catechism* blends common sense and pastoral sensitivity:

Sanctifying Sundays and holy days requires a common effort. Every Christian should avoid making unnecessary demands on others that would hinder them from observing the Lord's Day. Traditional activities (sport, restaurants, etc.), and social necessities (public services, etc.), require some people to work on Sundays, but everyone should still take care to set aside sufficient time for leisure. With temperance and charity the faithful will see to it that they avoid the excesses and violence sometimes associated with popular leisure activities. In spite of economic constraints, public authorities should ensure citizens a time intended for rest and divine worship. Employers have a similar obligation toward their employees. (*CCC* 2187)

Keeping the Lord's Day Holy: God's Time Management Tricks

Most of us complain that we don't have enough time. Our lives are so fast-paced (so goes the complaint, either to others or to ourselves) that they're almost out of control. We find ourselves frantically racing against the clock as often as not, and suffer the perennial torture of interior tension, stress, and pressure. Some also catch other time-related diseases: procrastination, boredom, addiction to certain sensual pleasures or wasteful pastimes (such as surfing the Internet). We all know that time is precious, but few of us are satisfied with how we manage it.

God invented time, so no one knows its ins and outs better than he does. In the Third Commandment, he presents us with the divine secret for successful time management, and he presents it not as a recommendation, but as a command—he knows we need it. Before looking at how to fulfill this commandment, however, ask yourself a question: *"Am I willing to trust God on this one?"* No matter how odd this commandment may seem, no matter how inconvenient, no matter how countercultural or even distasteful, are you willing to take the risk of following it? If so, read on.

The Original Sabbath: What Spiders Don't Know

"Remember to keep holy the Lord's Day" summarizes the divine directive for mastering your time. This implies that: (1) there is a day that belongs to the Lord, and (2) what we do on that day should somehow be different than what we do on other days.

Originally, the "Lord's Day" (the Jewish Sabbath) corresponded with the seventh day of the week, and it made its appearance at the very beginning of history. Genesis tells us: "Since on the seventh day God was finished with the work he had been doing, he rested on the seventh day.... So God blessed the seventh day and made it holy, because on it he rested from all the work he had done in creation" (2:2–3). God worked for six days and rested on the seventh. Man was created in the image of God, so he should follow the same pattern.

A simple explanation of the Lord's Day, but also profound: Woven right into the fabric of human nature, right into the tapestry of the space-time continuum, is the rhythm of work and leisure. Leisure, rest from our labors, is a requirement of human nature. Leisure involves the cultivation of relationships, of family unity (this is especially emphasized by the Church), refreshing and playful activity, relaxation, enjoyment of beauty (natural and artistic), and friendship. Such activities liken us to God, who rested on the seventh day, and distinguish us from the rest of creation, which keeps on working 24/7 (spiders don't take Sundays off to go on a family picnic). The Lord's Day "is a day of protest against the servitude of work and the worship of money" (*CCC* 2172).

But the Israelites had another reason to set aside a day for the Lord. "You shall remember that you were a servant in the land of Egypt, and the LORD your God brought you out thence with a mighty hand and an outstretched arm; therefore the LORD your God commanded you to keep the sabbath day" (Deuteronomy 5:15). We owe our existence to God, and taking a day off from "making a living" is an appropriate way to acknowledge that. But we also owe him our salvation. If Christ had not come, we would still be stuck in our sins; we would have no hope for heaven, for reaching the fullness of our human vocation (that is, to live in communion with God). He restored what our sin had destroyed, and he keeps restoring it, keeps administering his forgiveness. On the Lord's Day, therefore, we not only enjoy the rejuvenating power of leisure, but we also come together as God's people to give him thanks, rendering him, as is only right and fair, "outward, visible, public, and regular worship" (*CCC* 2176).

Sunday's Work

When Jesus Christ rose from the dead, he gave us yet another reason to "keep holy the Lord's Day." Since it was the first day of the week (the day after the Jewish Sabbath), it called to mind the day of creation (the first day of history). Since it marked his conquest of sin and death, it recalled the Exodus from Egypt, and since it was also the eighth day (the day after the seventh day, the last day of creation), it marked the beginning of his New Creation, which will culminate in the eternal Sabbath rest of the new heavens and the new earth at the end of time. Thus the Lord's Day migrated from Saturday to Sunday.

If we are seeking first God's kingdom and banking on him to lead us to the happiness we long for, we will show it by celebrating the Lord's Day in a way that will please him. We will follow the Church's precepts by our heartfelt attendance at the celebration of the Eucharist with our local Catholic community (not squeezing it in on Saturday afternoon so that we can sleep in on Sunday) and by refraining from our normal work duties—even if it means planning ahead and getting those nasty chores done on Friday and Saturday. We will link our leisure activities to our most important relationships—those of the family—and to our active love for God and neighbor, not mindlessly giving in to the secular rhythm of leisure on Friday and Saturday nights (and recovery in front of the TV on Sunday). We will show that we are God's children by living his day in a spirit of gratitude, charity, joy, and hope for the dawn of our eternal day of rest.

How exactly we live it out will depend on our own creativity and initiative, but the fact that we need to do it (for the health of our relationship with God and the health of our own souls) and that God commands us to do it is incontrovertible. Unavoidable circumstances often hinder us from living out the Lord's Day as we would like to; the Church understands that, as does God. But just as often we don't even make an effort. If we don't, we have no right to complain about stress and anxiety (God will just say, "I told you so!"). God invented time, and we would be wise to follow his weekly rhythm if we want to make good use of the little bit of it that comprises our lifetime.

CAN TRUTHS FROM OTHER RELIGIONS BE INTEGRATED INTO CATHOLICISM?

This is a great question, especially for today's world, where religious tolerance is seen by many as a universal value. Sometimes we can confuse openness and respect for believers in other religions with the sin of religious indifference, which consists either in ignoring the authentic demands of religion or in believing that all religions are the same. This question also addresses the connection between doctrine and practice. What we believe about God, ourselves, and the world affects how we behave and the choices we make. So let's start by clarifying the doctrine a bit, and then finish with some comments on the practical side.

Here is what the *Catechism* actually says about the "goodness and truth" found in non-Christian religions:

> The Catholic Church recognizes in other religions that search, among shadows and images, for the God who is unknown yet near since he gives life and breath and all things and wants all men to be saved. Thus, the Church considers all goodness and

truth found in these religions as "a preparation for the Gospel and given by him who enlightens all men that they may at length have life." (*CCC* 843)

In other words, human nature is the same for all people, and so all people experience, even in this fallen world, a yearning to reconnect with God, to live in communion with God. And this is why all people also experience the difficulty, the challenge, the obstacles involved in that search: Our human nature is fallen, and we need a savior. These are common elements in every religion. This is why different religions share so many commonalities and why many aspects of non-Christian religious are in harmony with Christianity.

In the very next paragraph, however, the *Catechism* makes a clarifying statement:

In their religious behavior, however, men also display the limits and errors that disfigure the image of God in them: "Very often, deceived by the Evil One, men have become vain in their reasonings, and have exchanged the truth of God for a lie, and served the creature rather than the Creator. Or else, living and dying in this world without God, they are exposed to ultimate despair." (*CCC* 844, quoting *Lumen Gentium*, 16)

In other words, although our common, fallen human nature universally searches for the way back to God, that same wounded nature creates a tendency for us to get lost and take dangerous and dead-end paths.

The Christian Difference
This is precisely why God himself intervened. His love and mercy moved him to come to our aid, to lead us along a sure path of return to communion with him and the happiness that we were created for. He did this through what is called revelation: God's own explanation of himself, the world, and how we can attain salvation. Revelation culminated in the

incarnation of the Second Person of the Trinity, Jesus Christ. Christ's work and teaching differs essentially from every other religion. It is God's effort to reach out to man, not just man's effort to reach up to God.

Consequently, the teaching and practice of the Catholic Church is unique; it's qualitatively different from those of other religions. Jesus is our standard, the sure standard by which we judge the truth, goodness, and utility of all other doctrines and traditions. The spiritual life, in other words, is not a smorgasbord. If we just pick and choose whichever practices we happen to like, we have no guarantee that we will avoid dangerous pitfalls (the "limits and errors" referenced by the *Catechism*).

Prayer traditions from other religions, therefore, may be able to harmonize with Christianity, but in order to do so they need to be purified and appropriately grafted into the authentic spiritual vine, Christ himself. That can only happen with the guidance of the Holy Spirit through his chosen instrument, the Church.

A final observation: It is often frustrating to find Catholics searching energetically for exciting new spiritual practices, but looking everywhere except within the incredibly rich and abundant traditions of their own Catholic Church.

WHAT IS GOD'S WILL REGARDING SUFFERING?

The spiritual life is, in its most basic elements, nothing less than a following of Christ, an imitation of him. And his very food—the thing he hungered for that nourished and strengthened him—was "to do the will of him who sent me" (John 4:34). The phrase "God's will" can cause confusion, however, unless we identify two broad subcategories: God's will can be either indicative or permissive.

God's Indicative Will

God can indicate that he wants us to do certain things—this is his indicative will. In this category we find the Ten Commandments, the commandments of the New Testament (such as, "Love one another as I have loved you" [John 15:12], "Go therefore and make disciples of all the nations" [Matthew 28:19]), the commandments and teachings of the Church (such as fasting on Good Friday), the responsibilities of our state in life, and specific inspirations of the Holy Spirit (for instance, when Blessed Teresa of Calcutta was inspired to start a new religious order to serve the poorest of the poor).

The field of God's indicative will is vast. It touches all the normal activities and relationships of every day, which are woven into the tapestry of moral integrity and faithfulness to our life's calling, plus the endless possibilities of the works of mercy, thus obeying the commandment to "love your neighbor as yourself" (Mark 12:31).

Yet God's will not only consists in what we do, but also in how we do it, which opens up the whole arena of growth in Christian virtue. We can wash the dishes (responsibilities of our state in life) with resentment and self-pity or with love, care, and supernatural joy. We can attend Sunday Mass apathetically and reluctantly or with conviction, faith, and attention. We can drive to work seething at the traffic jams or we can exercise patience. More often than not, when we ask ourselves, "What is God's will for me?" God's indicative will is crystal clear.

God's Permissive Will

But the phrase "God's will" also touches another category of life experience: suffering. Suffering, of one type or another, is our constant companion as we journey through this fallen world. God has revealed that suffering was not part of his original plan, but rather was the offspring of original sin, which ripped apart the harmony of God's creation. His indicative will to our first parents in the Garden of Eden was "but of the tree of the knowledge of good and evil you shall not eat" (see Genesis 2:17). They disobeyed. Human nature fell; creation fell; evil attained a certain predominance in the human condition, giving rise to "the overwhelming misery which oppresses men and their inclination towards evil and death" (*CCC* 403).

Here is where the distinction between God's indicative and permissive will comes in. God did not desire or command Adam and Eve to rebel against his plan, but he did permit them to do so. Likewise, throughout human history, God does not will evil to happen (and its consequence, suffering), but he does permit it. He certainly didn't explicitly will the Holocaust, for example, but on the other hand, he permitted it.

The question of why God permits some evil and the suffering that comes from it, even the suffering of innocents, is an extremely hard question to answer. Only the Christian faith as a whole gives a satisfactory response to it, a response that can only penetrate our hearts and minds through prayer, study, and the help of God's grace (see *CCC* 309). St. Augustine's short answer is worth mentioning. He wrote that if God permits evil to affect us, it is only because he knows that he can use it to bring about a greater good. We may not see that good right away; we may not see it at all during our earthly journey, in fact, but Christ's resurrection is the promise that God's omnipotence and wisdom are never trumped by the apparent triumphs of evil and suffering.

How Long Is Too Long?
You can know the will of God in your life through the commandments and the responsibilities of your calling (God's indicative will) and through the circumstances outside of your control that God allows (God's permissive will). Physical suffering is typically a circumstance that's out of your control; it would most likely fit into the category of God's permissive will.

Pray Freely, Accept God's Answer, and Live with Mystery
First, praying to be delivered from suffering is fine. It is one of the fruitful responses to suffering, because through that prayer we exercise our faith, hope, and love for God, along with the precious virtues of humility and perseverance. Jesus prayed for deliverance in Gethsemane. St. Paul prayed to be delivered from the thorn in his flesh (see 2 Corinthians 12:7). But this prayer of petition should always be offered with a condition: "Lord,

let me be healed of this affliction, if it be your will." We have to trust that if his answer to our prayer is no or not yet, that answer flows from his infinite love and wisdom, even if we don't particularly like it.

Second, as long as God has not healed you, either through a miracle or through the natural, prudent steps that you have taken (medical attention, for example), we know that he is still permitting your suffering. In that sense, it is his permissive will for you to continue bearing this cross. So, for now, this is part of God's will for you.

I say "part" because God's indicative will still applies. Even in the midst of our sufferings, we must strive to remember that by following the commandments and fulfilling the responsibilities of our state in life, we are glorifying God, building his kingdom, and following Christ. We should try to avoid letting our crosses blind us to the integral picture of our Christian discipleship (which includes continued participation in the sacraments, prayer, and loving others as God has loved us).

Third, on a very practical note, it is not always easy to know when to stop praying for a particular petition. In the Gospel, Jesus exhorts us to always "pray and not lose heart" (Luke 18:1), and even tells us a couple of parables to illustrate the point (see Luke 11 and 18). He also promises: "Ask, and it will be given you" (Matthew 7:7). And yet, St. Paul had the experience of asking for the thorn in his flesh to be removed—repeatedly—and God did not give him what he asked for.

There is a mystery here. St. Augustine explains that God sometimes refrains from giving us the specific thing we ask for because he wants to give us something better; he wants to respond to a deeper desire from which the specific petition flows.

Learning from St. Paul and a Practical Tip

St. Paul kept asking for the thorn in his flesh to be removed, until he received this answer from God: "My grace is sufficient for you, for my power is made perfect in weakness" (2 Corinthians 12:9). With that answer, Paul no longer felt a need to ask for healing.

As long as you feel in your heart the desire to be healed of your affliction, continue to bring your petition to the Lord. But in order to avoid becoming obsessed with or confused by the painful situation and God's mysterious response, perhaps it would be helpful to make your petition in the form of an established devotion. For example, you can make the Nine First Fridays devotion for this intention. Or you could do a novena to St. Pio Pietrelcina or to Our Lady of Good Remedy during the first nine days of every month. By circumscribing your petition for healing within an established devotion of some kind, you can be at peace that you are doing your part (persevering and not losing heart), while not letting your struggle disturb or dominate all the other aspects of your Christian discipleship.

WHAT ARE INDULGENCES?

The issue of indulgences is an area of difficulty for many people. In fact, it was one of the sparks that started the tragic blaze of the Protestant Reformation, a blaze that incinerated the cultural and religious unity of Christendom starting back in the 1500s.

An indulgence is simply a specific manifestation of God's grace, one that the Church offers to us as a concrete way show our love for the Lord and for our neighbor. An indulgence can only be attained with the intention of attaining it. So, if I were to lift my mind to God in the midst of my workday, I would not receive an indulgence for doing that unless I consciously intended to receive it. But I want to be very clear about something here. Indulgences are not the only spiritual benefits out there. Any time we engage in any of the spiritual exercises (reading sacred Scripture, praying the Stations of the Cross, saying specific prayers), we give glory to God and bring ourselves and our world into contact with the rushing stream of redeeming grace flowing from Christ's cross. Even if I am not intending to receive an indulgence, therefore, these spiritual practices are worthwhile, and God will reward them and utilize them to build up his kingdom. Through prayer and sacrifice, we become channels of God's grace, and an indulgence is a manifestation of that grace. There's no need to go indulgence hunting! If this practice doesn't resonate in your heart, don't worry. Continue to pray and seek the face of Christ in all you do, and let God take care of the rest.

A Touch of History

In the first centuries of the Church, confession and penance were much more public than they are now. It wasn't until the sixth century that the Irish monks really began to popularize individual, private confession. Until that era, it was more common for Christians who had fallen into grave sin to make their confession in front of the bishop and the entire congregation, and to be assigned a visible penance. For example, a public sinner might be required to wear some kind of penitential garb and stay in the back of the church during Mass for six months or even an entire year. Only at the end of that period of penance would he be admitted back into full communion with the Church.

Even during those early centuries, however, the practice of indulgences was emerging. For example, if a believer caved in under pressure of persecution and publicly denied his faith, it was considered the grave sin of apostasy. If that believer repented, he would be given a hefty penance. But that penance could be lessened if he visited a future martyr or confessor who was being held in prison for their faith. The believer would get this holy person to sign an affidavit by which he would express his desire to apply the merits of his sacrifice to the believer's penance. The believer then would bring this document to the bishop, and some or all of his penance could be remitted.

After the period of the Roman persecutions, obtaining this kind of remission of penance through the merits of the saints continued. Thus, the practice of indulgences emerged. Until recently, the relative value of the different indulgences was still expressed by correlating them to certain amounts of days—this harkens back to the early Church and its public penances, which were assigned for specific periods of time. Today this method of expressing the relative value of indulgences has been simplified. Instead of specific numbers of days, we just have partial or plenary (full) indulgences.

The Church's Favor

We really don't have the final say about how much benefit is bestowed when we obtain an indulgence. God is the final arbiter, and since only he can see our hearts, only he can see how pure is our love, our intention, and our detachment from sin—all of which are factors that contribute to the fruitfulness of any spiritual exercise we undertake.

Generally speaking (and it's always dangerous to generalize), our culture has lost a keen sense of sin. We tend to belittle the reality of sin and the seriousness of its consequences. This is partially a result of the influence of modern, secular psychology, which attributes blame not to free choice but to subconscious influences and tendencies. But our faith teaches us that there is only one thing in the universe more horrible than a venial sin, and that is a mortal sin. Sin is rebellion against God. Every sin is an attempt to destroy the universe. It is spiritual self-mutilation. It is spiritual chainsaw-massacring. When we spread lies about someone, for example, we actually upset the order of the cosmos; we do lasting damage to souls—our own and others'—souls that were created for eternal life and redeemed by Christ on the cross. Sin is a spiritual suicide-bomber attack.

If we really perceived the gravity of sin, we would more readily perceive the real need for penance and reparation. Then we would better understand the wisdom and the gentle love of God expressed in giving the Church the beautiful practice of indulgences. Through this practice, God offers us a concrete way to help right wrongs in the spiritual realm, to pour out spiritual balm on spiritual wounds, and to reestablish spiritual peace in war-torn souls.

An indulgence is simply a favor granted by the Church—to which, remember, Christ gave the "keys of the kingdom" and the power to bind and loose on earth and in heaven (see Matthew 16:19).

By means of this favor, the Church applies the merits won by Christ and the saints to repair the damage that sins cause to our soul. We don't obtain God's forgiveness through an indulgence, rather we obtain the remission of what is traditionally called "temporal punishment" for sin. This is an important concept to consider. It connects both to the doctrine of indulgences and also that of purgatory.

A Trip to Purgatory

Imagine that a young man leaves home to go off and fight in a war. He is gone for a long time, and when he finally returns, his clothes are tattered, he's half-starved, he is caked with mud and covered with blood, his head is bandaged, both his legs are broken, and one arm is in a homemade sling.

But he is alive, and he has made his way home. Will he go right into the dining room where the family is having a birthday dinner? No. He is not fit for such a celebration, and he wouldn't even want to make an appearance in his unpleasant condition. He has to go and get cleaned up first; the doctors will have to look at him and set those broken bones and change those bandages; he'll have to get his strength back, and undergo physical therapy to recover from his injuries.

The process may take a while, and it will probably be uncomfortable, even painful. It may take a full year before he's 100 percent healthy and able to participate fully in family affairs. But in the end, he'll take his rightful seat at the family feast.

That temporary recovery period is like purgatory. Our life on earth is a spiritual war. Our selfishness and sins not only offend God (sins that confession removes, as God grants us his forgiveness), but they also do damage to our souls. They form and deepen spiritual habits, tendencies, and attitudes that are contrary to the Gospel. And that damage needs to be repaired; every last scrap of selfishness and sinfulness has to be removed, or purified, before we are able to live in the perfect intimacy with God that heaven requires.

This purification can happen either in this life, or after we die. If it happens after we die, it is called purgatory—the state in which all remaining selfishness is purged from our souls.

God Indulges in Mercy

Through the favor granted by an indulgence, God's mercy permits this purification to happen more quickly than otherwise. Instead of having to suffer through the purification oneself, in other words, purification is obtained through the suffering already undergone by Christ and the saints. Indulgences can't free souls from hell, but they can speed up the purification process for oneself or for souls in purgatory, by remitting this temporal punishment (the restorative purification) that personal sins create the need for. There are two types of indulgences: partial, which repairs some of the self-damage caused by sin, or plenary, which repairs all the damage.

The Church usually attaches indulgences to some act of piety, by which we can show our love for God and neighbor. Plenary indulgences always include a particular act of piety (like half an hour adoration of the Blessed Sacrament), plus confession within a week, Holy Communion, and prayers for the pope and his intentions. But they also require a complete interior detachment from sin. Sometimes it is hard for us to know if we are fully detached. But even if we are not, God will honor our prayers and faith in some way, perhaps through granting a partial indulgence.

Those Complicated Catholics

This all might seem a bit complicated. Why doesn't God just simplify things? We can never know all of God's reasons, but the doctrine of indulgences does reflect his wisdom in myriad ways.

First of all, it shows his justice. God longs to forgive all sinners and welcome them back into his friendship and his family. But it would be unfair to simply ignore the damage that sin does. Justice requires that the damage, including that done by the sinner to the sinner's own soul, be repaired.

But God is also merciful, so he allows us to help each other out, to bear each other's burdens, to contribute to the good of one another—both here on earth, and after death. Furthermore, the obvious benefit that indulgences give to souls in purgatory can motivate us to a deeper prayer life. I know one couple who structure their spiritual lives around obtaining a plenary indulgence every day. This keeps them on track—they have to pray daily and be receiving the sacraments regularly in order to obtain those indulgences. It adds objectivity to their spiritual life.

The bottom line, however, is charity. Obtaining indulgences for souls suffering in purgatory exercises true supernatural love for neighbors whom we may never meet until our family feast in heaven. And when we exercise true, supernatural love, it grows; nothing matters more than that.

Not Merely Popular Piety

It's important to clarify that indulgences are not merely an expression of popular piety. Expressions of popular piety—pilgrimages, novenas to saints, and prayer vigils—are encouraged by the Church insofar as they help some of us stay energetic in our pursuit of holiness, but they are entirely optional.

Even the rosary (probably the most popular of all) is optional, though it has been strongly recommended by every pope since the start of the twentieth century. Even approved Marian apparitions (Fatima, Lourdes, Guadalupe) are not an integral part of the Catholic faith. No Catholic has to believe in them or be devoted to them. They belong to what is known as private revelations.

But doctrines like the resurrection of Christ and the Immaculate Conception are *not* optional. They are integral parts of Divine Revelation, and knowingly rejecting them is a sin against faith. Indulgences are closer to this side of the spectrum; they are both a doctrine and a practice. In other words, believing in indulgences is not optional. It is taught by the teaching authority of the Church as a true doctrine, as integrally related to revelation. So, even if some of us don't like the doctrine and the practice, even if we don't try to obtain them, we must accept the truth of indulgences as part of our faith.

You can read more about what the Church says about indulgences in the *Catechism* (1471–1479).

WHAT IS A NOVENA?

A novena is a formalized vocal prayer extended over a specific amount of time. Vocal prayer is the kind of prayer where we use other people's words to address God and lift our hearts and minds to him. The Our Father is a vocal prayer, for example. The famous prayer attributed to St. Francis of Assisi, "Make me an instrument of your peace…" is a vocal prayer. You don't have to say these prayers out loud to make them vocal; rather, you just have to give voice to the words of the prayer (*voice* and *vocal* both come from the same Latin root: *voco, vocare*, which means "to speak out" or "to call"). We can recite the words of a vocal prayer in the silence of our hearts, or audibly. In either case, however, vocal prayers give us a channel for the desires and thoughts of our souls.

When we use this kind of prayer, we align our minds and hearts with the meaning of the words, giving God praise, renewing our faith and trust, asking him for things we need or desire, or all of the above. A good vocal prayer helps us connect with God. It also reinforces our Christian convictions: By giving words to good desires and expressions of love for God, we actually exercise those desires and that love, and when we exercise them they grow.

A novena is a vocal prayer, or series of vocal prayers, that you commit to praying over an extended period of time. These prayers are usually linked to a specific devotion (for instance, devotion to a particular saint) or liturgical celebration (a novena for Pentecost, for example). They are also very often linked to a specific intention—you can offer a novena as a way to petition God for the healing of a sick person or the conversion of someone who is far away from God. The words of the novena will reflect all of these factors. They will remind you of the meaning of the liturgical celebration, the virtues of a saint, or the goodness of God. And the combination of prayers will also, usually, give you a place to insert your personal petition.

It's important to remember, however, that novenas are not magic formulas. They are prayers. They are one way we can enter into conversation with God.

The History of Novenas

The most common period of time for praying a novena is nine days. The word *novena* actually comes from the Latin word for "nine." The nine-day period of prayer has its origin in the book of Acts. After Jesus' ascension into heaven, the apostles, the Blessed Virgin Mary, and some of Christ's other followers all joined in continuous prayer (Acts 1:14) for nine days, until the dramatic coming of the Holy Spirit on Pentecost. We know it was nine days because the ascension happened forty days after the resurrection (see Acts 1:3), and Pentecost was always celebrated fifty days after the Passover. The resurrection happened the day following the Passover, so we can do the math: 50-40-1=9. This period in which the fledgling Church "joined in continuous prayer" in anticipation of the promised coming of the Holy Spirit was the first novena. Through the centuries, the strict period of nine days has taken various forms, including the nine First Fridays devotion recommended by our Lord to St. Margaret Mary Alacoque and linked to the devotion to the Sacred Heart. Sometimes you even find local traditions of thirty-day or three-day novenas.

Why Pray a Novena?

In general, we pray novenas for the same reason that we pray at all: because God deserves our praise, and because we need his grace. Novenas are prayers, and all the benefits that prayer always brings are also brought by novenas. This particular form of prayer, however, has some special characteristics.

First, a novena provides a channel for strong spiritual sentiments or desires. Sometimes our souls are so full of sorrow, or anxiety, or hope, or thirst for holiness that it is hard for us to find the words to express ourselves. A novena gives us a vehicle for prayerful expression. A novena can be a powerful way to mourn the loss of a loved one, for example; a novena of Masses can be a beautiful way to commend that person's soul to God's mercy. In a crisis, a novena can channel our apprehension in a positive way—entrusting our deeply felt needs to God through the intercession of a saint, for example. Novenas put clear parameters around deep spiritual sentiments, enabling us to have confidence that we are keeping them in harmony with God and his will. In this way, they provide true comfort to our souls; they assure us that we are doing our part, so to speak, in response to particular needs of our own or those of others.

Second, they help us stay in sync with our spiritual family, the Church. By joining in the Divine Mercy Novena (from Good Friday to Divine Mercy Sunday), for example, we unite ourselves to millions of other Catholics all over the world who are engaged in the same prayer. By praying a novena before a major liturgical celebration like Christmas or Pentecost, we can prepare our souls to engage in that celebration more fruitfully and less superficially.

DO I NEED TO BECOME A CATHOLIC TO GO TO HEAVEN?

First, let me point out a major difference between being Catholic and being Protestant. One of the many beautiful things about the Eucharist (which Catholics receive in Holy Communion) is that it doesn't depend upon how we feel. Whether we are tired, angry, distracted, sad, confused—whatever we are feeling, we know with certainty that Jesus is truly present in the Eucharist and that he comes to us, gladly and fully of his generous grace, when we receive him in Holy Communion.

One reason that Communion's positive effect in our soul doesn't depend on how we feel is that Christ's presence in it is objectively real. It is not imaginary; it is not symbolic; it is not concocted by the level of our devotion. No! Jesus is truly present in the sacrament of the Eucharist because a validly ordained priest has celebrated the highest act of worship that our Lord left his Church: the Mass. During the Mass, the priest consecrates the bread and wine, and through the power of the Holy Spirit they become the Body and Blood of Jesus Christ. Not just anyone can celebrate the Mass, but only an ordained priest (through the special graces of apostolic succession under the authority of the See of St. Peter). The Holy Spirit established that requirement precisely because he wanted us to be able to be absolutely, objectively certain that Christ is truly present in the Eucharist.

And so, although receiving communion in a non-Catholic liturgy can be an experience of true devotion and deep prayer, nevertheless, you are not receiving the Body and Blood of our Lord as you can in the Catholic Church, and so you are not receiving the sacramental grace that comes with it.

What's the Next Step?

A person certainly should not convert to Catholicism if he or she has not come to the conviction that the Catholic Church is the Church that Christ founded, the Church with the fullness of truth and grace. But you don't have to sit around and wait passively for that conviction to come to you. It may come in a flash—that would be a special grace. Usually, though, conversion is a journey, a journey in which the Holy Spirit guides you into a deeper and deeper friendship with Jesus. And you get to the point where, because you love Jesus so much, you want to receive all that he wants to give you, including the unique guidance, grace, and fellowship that his Catholic Church offers. When non-Catholic Christians become Catholics, they leave nothing behind—they just get more stuff!

Just continue asking yourself, "What is the next step I can take to continue along this journey?" If you keep following one step after another, generously and courageously, the Holy Spirit will guide you surely into the very center of the burning fire of love of the Sacred Heart of Jesus. One possible next step for you could be to read about the journeys of other non-Catholic Christians who have become Catholics.

Getting to Heaven

Do you need to be a Catholic to go to heaven? Well, we can look at this from a couple of different perspectives. On the one hand, we can say that everyone in heaven is Catholic, because the Catholic Church is the Body of Christ and the family of God, and in heaven everyone will be members of the same family. But everyone who dies and goes to heaven isn't necessarily and formally a member of the Catholic Church. If God gave them sufficient light to see clearly that the Catholic Church was his true Church, and they purposely and repeatedly rejected that light and refused to become Catholic and never repented, then God will certainly not force them to live in his family for all eternity—he respects our freedom. Here is how the Catholic *Catechism* puts it (quoting one of the Church Councils):

> Basing itself on Scripture and Tradition, the Council teaches that the Church, a pilgrim now on earth, is necessary for salvation: the one Christ is the mediator and the way of salvation; he is present to us in his body which is the Church. He himself explicitly asserted the necessity of faith and Baptism, and thereby affirmed at the same time the necessity of the Church which men enter through Baptism as through a door. Hence they could not be saved who, knowing that the Catholic Church was founded as necessary by God through Christ, would refuse either to enter it or to remain in it.
>
> This affirmation is not aimed at those who, through no fault of their own, do not know Christ and his Church:

Those who, through no fault of their own, do not know the Gospel of Christ or his Church, but who nevertheless seek God with a sincere heart, and, moved by grace, try in their actions to do his will as they know it through the dictates of their conscience—those too may achieve eternal salvation.

Although in ways known to himself God can lead those who, through no fault of their own, are ignorant of the Gospel, to that faith without which it is impossible to please him, the Church still has the obligation and also the sacred right to evangelize all men. (*CCC* 846–848)[9]

CAN NON-CHRISTIANS GO TO HEAVEN?

This question has generated reams of theological speculation, argument, and even bitter diatribes. In fact, it became so problematic back in the eighties and nineties that the Congregation for the Doctrine of the Faith, under the leadership of then-Cardinal Joseph Ratzinger, actually published (with the full approval of St. John Paul II) a thorough treatment of the issue, called *Dominus Iesus*. (You may want to read it, but give yourself some time and a full pot of tea; it is rich, but somewhat long and somewhat dense).

Christ Is the Bridge

The short answer to your question is this: Anyone who ends up in heaven is a member of the Church. Heaven is communion with God; it is being a fully mature member of his family. The only bridge to heaven is Christ—he is the only Savior, and only his self-sacrifice on the cross opened the gates of heaven and atoned for human sin.

Now, in theory it is possible to cross a bridge without knowing the name of that bridge. You can even cross a bridge in the fog, for example, without realizing that you are crossing a bridge. This is an image that can help us understand how a person could be saved, could enter heaven and become a full member of God's family for all eternity, without being a Catholic here on earth. The condition for that, according to Church teaching, is that individuals like this, through no fault of their own, "do not know the Gospel of Christ or his Church, but who nevertheless seek God with a sincere heart, and moved by grace, try in their actions to do his will as they know it" (*CCC* 847).

Obviously, you and I are incapable of judging whether some are seeking God with a sincere heart, or whether their non-membership in the Catholic Church is "through no fault of their own." Furthermore, through God's providence, we have come to know the name of the bridge; we have been given, by the sheer gift of God's grace, the wisdom for salvation through faith in Jesus Christ. The greatest act of love we can make toward our neighbor is to share that faith with those haven't yet received it or who have lost it. As Benedict XVI affirmed in his first public homily as pope: "The purpose of our lives is to reveal God to men.... There is nothing more beautiful than to know Him and to speak to others of our friendship with Him." This is the meaning behind what the Church has always called—and still calls—the "missionary mandate" (*CCC* 849): "Having been divinely sent to the nations that she might be 'the universal sacrament of salvation,' the Church, in obedience to the command of her founder and because it is demanded by her own essential universality, strives to preach the Gospel to all men."[10]

Means vs. Ends

The main point of recent discussions about these truths has to do more with the way we approach this missionary mandate, not its validity. Since the Second Vatican Council, the Church has made a concerted effort to reach out to people of other religions in a respectful way—respecting them as people, respecting the search for truth and salvation that their religion represents—and not with a condemning tone.

But make no mistake about it. Although we are called to respect all people and their search for religious truth, Jesus Christ alone remains the

Way, the Truth, and the Life, and all salvation comes from him "through the Church which is his Body" (*CCC* 846).

WHY IS HOLY COMMUNION ONLY FOR CATHOLICS?

Receiving Holy Communion is a deeply personal encounter with Jesus Christ, who is truly present under the appearances of bread and wine within Christ's family of the Church. When Jesus gives himself to us in Holy Communion, he is saying in effect: "I know you and I love you. I long to share your life and to allow you to share my life. I want you with me, and I want my grace to heal, strengthen, enlighten, and guide your difficult journey through this fallen world. I give you this spiritual nourishment as a sign of my love for you and my commitment to you. All that I lived, taught, and suffered, I did for you."

An Intimate Encounter

When we receive Holy Communion, we are accepting Christ's love and Christ's grace. That includes accepting all that he has taught, and all that his Church teaches, about the meaning of life and the path to fuller and fuller union with (this is what *communion* means) our Lord and Savior here on earth, and to a complete union with him forever in heaven. When we receive him, we are telling him: "Lord, I believe in you, and in all you have taught, and in all you have done for me. I believe in your Church, through which you give me this Blessed Sacrament. I long to follow you more closely. I long for my life to give you glory and to be a mirror of your goodness in this dark world. I promise to do everything I can to obey your commandments, since that is how you have asked me to show you my love. I want to live in true friendship with you, today, tomorrow, and forever."

Avoiding a Lie

Now, someone who does not accept what the Catholic Church teaches about faith and morals cannot actually say those things. They cannot be in full communion with Christ in the Catholic Church, because the Catholic Church believes that Christ continues to act in the world through his Church. A Lutheran, an Episcopalian, or a Buddhist, for instance, does not accept all the basic teachings of the Gospels as explained in the Catholic *Catechism*, and so they are not in communion with Christ in his Church—if they did accept those teachings, they would become Catholic. So, for someone in that position to receive Holy Communion in the Catholic Church is, in a sense, for them to say something that they really don't believe (such as, "I am in communion with Christ and his Catholic Church"); it's a kind of lie.

If someone who does believe what the *Catechism* teaches about faith and morals (and the *Catechism* is simply a systematic explanation of what Jesus taught in the Gospels and the Holy Spirit teaches in the rest of the Scriptures) but refuses to live by that teaching, they would also be contradicting themselves by receiving Holy Communion. Someone who is having an affair, for example, would need to repent of the sin, confess it, and make a firm resolution to break off the affair before receiving Holy Communion. An affair is a grave sin against marriage, against God's plan for marriage, and against God's plan for the people having the affair. To receive Communion without repenting from and confessing that sin is like saying to Jesus, "I want to follow you, but I think you are wrong about the meaning of marriage and the evil of adultery, so I am just going to keep doing my own thing in that area." It's a contradiction; it's saying that I am in communion with Christ, but then, in my next breath, turning around and rejecting him, slapping him in the face. It's, again, in a certain sense, a lie.

St. Paul was very clear about the reverence and right-heartedness required for worthy reception of Holy Communion: "Whoever, therefore, eats the bread or drinks the cup of the Lord in an unworthy manner will be guilty of profaning the body and blood of the Lord. Let a man examine himself, and so eat of the bread and drink of the cup" (1 Corinthians 11:27–28). Let us all pray that we will receive Jesus with the love he longs for, and help others do the same. He wants that—passionately.

Notes

1. Pope Benedict XVI, "Mass for the Inauguration of the Pontificate of Pope Benedict XVI: Homily of His Holiness Benedict XVI," April 24, 2005, http://www.vatican.va/holy_father/benedict_xvi/homilies/documents/hf_ben-xvi_hom_20050424_inizio-pontificato_en.html.
2. Mother Teresa, *Come Be My Light: The Private Writings of the Saint of Calcutta,* Brian Kolodiejchuk, ed. (New York: Image, 2009).
3. Letter of July 6, 1591, quoted in *St. John of the Cross,* ed. E. Allison Peers (London: Cambridge University Press).
4. Pope Benedict XVI, General Audience, June 3, 2009.
5. T.S. Eliot, *Four Quartets* (Boston: Mariner, 1968), p. 13.
6. *Imitation of Christ,* chapter one.
7. John Paul II's 1998 Apostolic Letter *Dies Domini,* 47.
8. *United States Catholic Catechism for Adults* (Washington, D.C.: United States Conference of Catholic Bishops, 2006), 364.
9. Quoting *Lumen Gentium,* 14, 15, *Ad Gentes,* 7; referencing Mark 15:16, John 3:5, Denzinger-Schönmetzer, 3866–3872, Hebrews 11:6, and 1 Corinthians 9:16.
10. "Mass for the Inauguration of the Pontificate of Pope Benedict XVI: Homily of His Holiness Benedict XVI," St. Peter's Square, April 24, 2005.

About the Author

Fr. John Bartunek, L.C., S.T.D., received his B.A. in history from Stanford University in 1990. He comes from an evangelical Christian background and became a member of the Catholic Church in 1991. He was ordained a Catholic priest in 2003 and earned his doctorate in moral theology in 2010. He is the author of *The Better Part* and *Inside the Passion*.